Transforming Communities

Transforming Communities

Re-imagining the Church for the 21st Century

STEVEN CROFT

DARTON · LONGMAN + TODD

First published in 2002 by
Darton, Longman and Todd Ltd
1 Spencer Court
140–142 Wandsworth High Street
London SW18 4JJ

ISBN 0-232-52465-4

A catalogue record for this book is available from the British Library.

Set in 9.5/12.75pt Palatino
Designed and produced by Sandie Boccacci
using QuarkXPress on an Apple PowerMac

Printed and bound in Great Britain by
Page Bros, Norwich, Norfolk

Contents

PART THREE

Nurturing the Vision:
The Church in Scripture and Tradition   103

Preface

Transforming Communities is an attempt to re-imagine and find a direction for shaping the life of the local church around the life of small missionary communities.

The book is in four parts. Chapter One stands alone at the head of the book as a paradigm story which introduces its main theme. It is not based on a real situation but is about how things might develop. You should imagine the story being told to a group of people about fifty years in the future, describing a change that began to come about in the way that we are church. The story seems to work well when it is read aloud, sometimes with a pause for discussion in between each section. It is not meant to be a perfect representation of how things might be – you may find things you want to criticise as well as to affirm.

Part Two, 'Seeing Clearly' (Chapters Two to Six), outlines the main thesis with an analysis of the situation we face; a look at how new vision grows; some alternatives we encounter; and an overview of what transforming communities might be like and the resources on which we can draw. I hope this part of the book might be read and discussed by all concerned with the future life and ministry of the local church and that it might provide material for local ministry teams, PCCs, parish away days, clergy chapters, fraternals, and so on. There are one or two questions at the end of each chapter designed to act as starters for this discussion – but feel free to range more widely.

Part Three (Chapters Seven to Ten) tests the thesis of transforming communities as a way forward against a theological understanding of what it means to be the church. These chapters may well be useful to the groups who will read Part One. I hope that this section may also be useful to all kinds of small groups who may be trying to put these ideas (and similar ones) into practice. Again, you will find a short list of questions at the end of each chapter to help guide discussion.

Finally, Part Four (Chapters Eleven and Twelve) aims to give some practical guidance for churches and ministry teams seeking to develop small missionary communities as building blocks of local church life. These chapters are intended as a kind of simple manual and may also be useful as a training resource both for a co-ordinating group and for leaders of transforming communities.

The book has been written over a period of just over a year but builds upon about twenty years' experience and reflection as a curate, vicar, diocesan mission consultant and theological educator. It is by no means the last word on any subject, but is offered in the hope that the ideas here will stimulate others in their reflection and the development of local church life. The opportunity in my present post to interact with a wide range of dioceses, ministers and students in the Methodist and Roman Catholic Churches, clergy, lay ministers and ordinands has been invaluable in gaining perspective for the task. I am writing from an English and Anglican perspective but hope that the insights here will prove useful in other contexts.

The scope of *Transforming Communities* is already quite large, embracing an analysis of the present situation, theological reflection on the church and practical guidelines for a way forward. I am conscious that there are some omissions, such as how to adapt the ideas here for particular groups within the church, such as children and young people, and for particular theological traditions and social settings. Lack of space has prevented my doing justice to this. Other themes I have dealt with elsewhere. The view of the role of the ordained implied in this book is entirely consistent with the picture given in *Ministry in Three Dimensions*[1] and implies something of a shift in orientation to include a larger measure of both collaborative work and the oversight of small communities. The picture of evangelism, nurture and growth is, again, entirely consistent with my earlier material on that theme.[2] Much of the Emmaus material will provide an excellent resource for the kind of groups envisaged here.

Thanks are due to all those who have listened to the material along the way, particularly during the genesis of the book itself. Chapter Two was originally delivered at the Lichfield Diocesan Clergy Conference in April 2001. Chapter One has been tried out in whole or in part on incumbents in Durham Diocese, the post-ordination training group in Sheffield in November 2001, and ordinands in Cranmer Hall. An early version of Chapter Five was tested on my colleagues here and significantly amended in con-sequence. Much of the material in Part Two was road-tested in the course I teach in Cranmer Hall on Christian Leadership. All of these occasions and others have generated very useful feedback. The Bible studies at the beginning of Chapters Two, Three and Four have been published by CPAS in their *Church Leadership Magazine*.

I owe a particular debt to a range of individuals. Those who have taken the time and trouble to read parts of the manuscript and make detailed comments on the draft in the midst of busy lives have been enormously helpful. Here I would thank especially Rita Acarnley, Philip King, Michael Turnbull and Gavin Wakefield. Others have acted as conversation partners throughout, have suggested readings and have been invaluable as a source of references, in particular my colleagues in St John's College: Alan Bartlett, Mark Bonnington, Jocelyn Bryan, Stephen Burns, Mark Cartledge, David Clough, Bob Fyall, Judy Hirst, Charles Read, Robert Scott-Biggs, Chloe Starr, Geoffrey Stevenson, Stephen Sykes, Helen Thorp, Roger Walton and David Wilkinson. Janet Hodgson, Rob Marshall and Alison and Frank White all commented helpfully on the original proposal. Anthony Clegg and Steve Lee, on sabbatical here this year, gave very valuable feedback as part of our regular conversations. Robin McKenzie and Rob Brown, with others in training, were helpful sounding boards on social capital and biblical models of the church. John Plant in Leicester Diocese was the first to read some of the manuscript and the means of preserving the first draft of Chapters Two to Six when my laptop was stolen. Still others have helped by encouragement and through prayer – not least Gillian Belford, who had many other things going on in her life at the time. My colleagues Margaret Trivasse and Val Strickland helped preserve time and space for writing. The team at Darton, Longman and Todd have been a pleasure to work with. My family, as ever, have given every support.

I hope you enjoy *Transforming Communities* and pray that you will find it useful as a way of reflecting on the past, present and future shape of being church.

STEVEN CROFT
March 2002

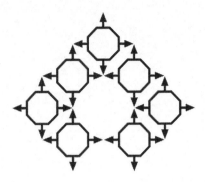

PART ONE

A Story

1

A Story

Once upon a time in a place far away there was a church.

On Sundays the people who made up the church came to a special building. Some came from very near and others from a distance. A few came every week but many came to the building less often now because their lives were busy. The special building had rows of long benches called pews all facing in the same direction. One or two people would sit in each pew. A special person called a vicar stood at the front of the building and led the worship service. In winter, the building was cold and the people rarely took off their coats. They sang together, listened to the Scriptures and prayed for the world. Some exchanged a sign of the peace but a few refused to join in. All of them shared in Holy Communion. Some of the people would stay behind after the service for a few minutes to talk to the vicar or to share a cup of weak coffee. Then they would each go to their own homes. For the most part, the people who came to the church had been coming for a long time. Very occasionally, a new person or family came but they did not usually stay long.

Some of the people who went to the church sometimes saw each other during the week at special events called committees. The committees normally met in cold, draughty places and people some-times kept their coats on there as well. The vicar was normally chair of the committee and said a prayer at the beginning. The committees talked together mainly about problems and difficulties: about the special building and about how to keep things going for another year. Sometimes the people argued with one another at the committees. During the week the vicar would call in to see people at their homes to chat and sometimes he would stay for a cup of tea. If any church members were poorly or in hospital he would visit them and pray for them.

Many of the people in the church thought they could remember a time when the building was full on Sundays and there were lots of children and younger people. They could remember too when the building was used on different days of the week and several times on Sunday. Many people used to come there to get married and to bring their children to be baptised. But that seemed a very long time ago. Most of the people who made up the church were quite old now. Some were sad that more people didn't come and they prayed for change. Some were afraid that the building may have to close. Many had simply become resigned to the way things were and carried on with their lives.

Things went on in this way for many years until the day came when the small church could no longer have its own vicar. In those days there were not enough to go round and sometimes one vicar would be shared by three or four churches or even more. At first the new shared vicar tried to take all the services and chair all the committees and visit all the people. This made some of the people cross because things were not done the way they liked. It also made the shared vicar quite poorly and made him wonder what to do.

Then, one day, the vicar invited the people in the church to a new kind of meeting which wasn't a committee. Only seven people could come.

'I've been trying to think about what it means to be a church,' said the new Vicar. 'I want to talk with you about it this evening. What do you think?'

Some of the people were confused and some were frightened but said nothing. One of the braver ones said: 'It means coming to the service on Sundays and sometimes coming to committees. When we are poorly, the vicar comes to see us.' The others all nodded.

'I know that's the way we've always done church,' said the Vicar in a kindly way. 'But that doesn't seem to be working any more. I'm too busy trying to do everything in four churches because I'm a shared vicar and that's made me poorly. Some of you are cross that I can't do everything. Nobody new is coming to church and nobody seems very happy.'

The little group nodded again but looked puzzled. 'But we don't know any other way,' they said.

'Listen to this,' said the Vicar, as he read them some verses from the Bible. 'This is what it says in the Acts of the Apostles about what the church used to be. See what you think.

> 'They devoted themselves to the apostles' teaching and fellow-ship, to the breaking of bread and prayers ... All who believed were together and had all things in common; they would sell their possessions and goods and distribute the proceeds to all, as any had need. Day by day, as they spent much time together in the temple, they broke bread at home and ate their food with glad and generous hearts, praising God and having the good-will of all the people. And day by day the Lord added to their number those who were being saved.'[1]

After the Vicar had read these words, the group was silent for some time. Heaven held its breath. Unseen angels stood on tiptoe around the room, glimpsing a different kind of future.

'It sounds as though they knew one another,' said one man in a puzzled voice.

'They spent time together,' said another.

'They prayed and helped each other,' said a third.

'People wanted to come and join them.'

'It sounds lovely,' sighed the youngest member of the group. 'I wish I could have been a Christian back then.'

'Do you think we could try and be more like that today?' asked the Vicar.

One man became angry and left the room without saying where he was going. But the others stayed and talked until late in the evening. Each of them voiced similar frustrations and a longing for something better. The group agreed to meet again the next week, this time in someone's home.

Over the months that followed, something new began to happen in the life of the little church. The small group that met during the week began to get to know one another in deeper ways. Just like the church in Acts, they began to meet in one another's homes, as we still do today. Week by week, they shared their stories and their lives; discovered worship and prayer together, and read God's word to one another.

With the gentle encouragement of the Vicar, different people began to share in the various parts of leading the group and contributing to its life. Some of them grew in confidence so much they were able to share in leading the services on Sundays.

Because the people knew one another, they were able to support one another quite naturally. A young married couple in the church had a new baby. Members of the group made meals and took them round. Everyone shared in the joy. An elderly member of the group had a fall and was taken to hospital. When the Vicar arrived, he found that two other people had already been to visit. When the Vicar came to the group one week looking very distressed, the group listened carefully to his feelings of anxiety about the future and several people offered helpful advice.

Other members of the church noticed a new life about this group. A few were suspicious but the next time a general invitation was given to others to come along, the group grew in size. In a way no one could quite understand, the sense of renewal and refreshing in the midweek meetings spilled over into Sunday worship. For the first time in many years, when people appeared in the congregation on Sundays they sensed the warmth of Christian fellowship and some began to attend the services regularly.

2

Six months after the group began to meet, the Vicar called them together with a new challenge. Everyone shared a meal together and a time of prayer before the Vicar began to speak.

'It's been an exciting journey,' he said, 'but I would like to take some time this evening to think about what has been happening to us as a group. Would anyone like to say anything about how you see things?'

'I would,' said Mary. 'My whole faith has been renewed.'

'I feel like I have a whole new family,' said Alice.

'Going to the service on Sundays is a different experience,' said Jim. 'I go now to be with my friends as well as to worship God.'

'I've done things I never thought I'd do in this group.'

'People at work have said there is something different about me over the last few months.'

Every member of the group had something good to say. 'That is very wonderful,' said the Vicar. 'I think we have learned a lot more about being church. It's taken six months but there is a sense that we are beginning to put into practice what we have learned in Acts. But this evening, I want to read another passage to you.'

The group was quiet and expectant. Some remembered the first evening they met. Others had heard the moment spoken of as they talked together. The Vicar began to read:

> 'Now in the church at Antioch there were prophets and teachers: Barnabas, Simeon who was called Niger, Lucius of Cyrene, Manaen, a member of the court of Herod the ruler, and Saul. While they were worshipping the Lord and fasting, the Holy Spirit said, "Set apart for me Barnabas and Saul for the work to which I have called them." Then after fasting and praying they laid hands on them and sent them off.[2]

'It's so good that we meet together,' said the Vicar. 'It's good that we are getting to know one another and that we can support each other. We are becoming a community. Through this new community our faith is being renewed. We are discovering each other's gifts as we meet together and we have welcomed new people to join us. But God calls us also to serve him and to live for him, individually and together. Unless we do that, I'm afraid that we will become inward looking and not be the church we are called to be. That is always a danger for God's people. I'd like us to think about what that might mean for us as individuals and as a group.'

'I like things the way they are,' said one person. 'I don't want things to change.'

There was silence in the room for some time. Heaven held its breath. Unseen angels stood around the room, again glimpsing different futures. Some were hopeful, others anxious.

'I like things the way they are as well,' said another, after some time. 'But I think we need this challenge. What we have has enriched our lives but that is so we can serve God and serve others.'

'The church in Acts didn't stay the same,' said another. 'God challenged them to move on so that more people could discover the gospel. Perhaps God is challenging us in the same way.'

The rest of the group agreed. Over the next three months there was a new element in their meetings. The members still came together to pray and to read God's Word and to support one another. But now they began to think individually and together about the different ways in which God might be calling them to share his love.

People took it in turns to bring to the meeting an area of concern at home or in their work or their life outside home. One person was a social worker and shared some general details about the different challenges at work. A young mum was struggling with her children. The group encouraged her by sharing experiences and one member talked with her about teaching her daughter to pray and eventually ended up babysitting from time to time. Another had been involved for years in fundraising for a local hospice. The next time there was an event, the whole group helped in some way by providing goods to sell or by turning up on the day.

Week by week, it seemed that people had more to talk about when they met and some members began to take new steps in helping others. After some time, at the Vicar's suggestion, the group began to pray together about discovering what God was calling them to do together. 'Even though we are all supporting each other in our life and work,' he said, 'it is important that we try and do something together because that is an important part of our life together.'

There were a number of suggestions for what this might be. Two of the group members had become involved in leading a very small midweek group for parents and toddlers which met on church premises. The small community decided to adopt this group as their mission project for the next year. Each time they met, they prayed for the life of the toddler group. One person managed the accounts. Another came and made the tea and played with the children. Another made posters and put them in doctors' surgeries. Once a term all the community members came and helped clean the toys. With the help of other members of the church, a crèche opened on Sunday mornings. With this kind of support, the parent and toddler group was able to expand, raise funds, buy new equipment and become a very valuable part of local life. After the year of support by the group, a number of the other carers were able to become involved in the life of the toddler group and there wasn't the same need for this kind of support, although there was always a strong link between the small community and the toddlers.

3

A whole year after the group first began to meet, part way through the mission project, the Vicar called them together for another review meeting. Again, the community had a sense of excitement and anticipation as the members gathered together. There were now fifteen people who came to most of the meetings and another group of five or six who were only able to attend from time to time. As they prepared to meet together, each took stock of how the life of the small community had grown and developed over the last twelve months.

Some time ago, the community had decided to meet once a fortnight in order to give time and space for the mission project and other concerns. Whenever they met together there was great joy and a sense of the presence of God. Different members took it in turns to lead the prayer and worship of the community. There was always a time of praise and thanksgiving, a time of listening to God through his word and a time of intercession. Different members again took responsibility for leading the group in its study and learning. There was a common sense of growing in faith and discipleship. The Book of Acts had a special place in their common journey. Almost every month, someone new came to visit and several had joined the group. One person had become a Christian and the group had shared in her baptism and confirmation service. Two or three people had developed a more pastoral role and took the lead in ensuring members of the group were supported during particular times of difficulty. Others took the lead in the mission projects and helping the community reflect on that aspect of its life. The Vicar was still a member of the community but, for the last few months, he had been coming less often and the group had been guided in his absence by three lay members.

'So much has happened to us over the last year,' said the Vicar. 'There is so much for which we should thank God. We have learned to share our lives and to share in God's mission. Together we encourage one another to love God and to love our neighbour. However, there is another small step I believe we still need to take.'

A stillness settled onto the gathering.

'In the Book of Acts we read how the apostles began new churches. Those churches mostly met in people's homes, just as we do today, as well as in more public places when they were allowed to do so. But the apostles were always being called by God to move on to different places, to preach the gospel and to form new communities of Christians. That meant they had to appoint new ministers to guide and protect the life of small communities in every place where the church began.

'I believe that is the point we have reached today in the life of this small community. It is time for me to hand over responsibility for this group to ministers who are suited to the task. This is part of what the Apostle Paul says in Acts when he is handing over responsibility to the ministers in Ephesus: "Keep watch over yourselves and over all the flock, of which the Holy Spirit has made you overseers, to shepherd the church of God that he obtained with the blood of his own Son."'[3]

There was silence in the crowded room. Only one angel stood unseen and watched the gathering. The others were at a distance. This angel was young and not yet fully grown: part hopeful, part hesitant. Looking forward but glancing over his shoulder for support.

'Do you think we can manage on our own?' asked one person.

'Yes, I do,' said the Vicar. 'We have seen over the last year that God will provide all the gifts that are needed.'

'What about when there are problems?' asked another.

'There will always be problems,' said the Vicar. 'I will still be in the background, supporting the ministers who lead the groups.'

'We will miss you being here,' said a third.

'Thank you. I will miss you as well,' said the Vicar. 'I have gained a great deal through this group and learned many new things about myself and about serving God. I know things may be hard but I also think the life of this community will go from strength to strength.'

Discussion turned to the practical arrangements that needed to be made. The Vicar asked the group to pray about the people who should be asked to lead. He also strongly recommended that the single community should become two separate groups.

'This is now a very large gathering,' he said. 'It's becoming hard to find places big enough to meet in. There is no room for new people and we have lost some of the closeness we knew in the first six months.'

The community reflected on both of these questions and followed the Vicar's advice. After prayer and consultation, two new ministers were appointed for each of the new communities. All of them had been active in sharing in guiding the group over the last few months. They were commissioned in the main Sunday morning worship service. Between them, the new ministers discussed with the group who might be part of each new group, together with four or five new people who wanted to take this opportunity to be involved in what was happening.

A month later the original group met for the last time for a service of Holy Communion led by the Vicar. There were many moving testimonies to what God had done. The new groups and the ministers were prayed for. There was a sense of sadness but also excitement that God was doing a new thing.

The Vicar met with the four ministers regularly over the next few months. As a small group, they reviewed each meeting, encouraged one another, prayed together and tried to discern what the Spirit was doing in each community. As things turned out, the two groups were very different. One felt like a continuation of the original community. There was an initial sense of loss because some friends were not present. However, the meetings continued much as before. The new members were quickly incorporated into the ongoing life of the group. This group continued with the original mission project of supporting the toddler group but was already beginning to think about a new common call. However, the second group was very different. The members were mainly those who had been slightly on the edge of the original group together with new people who had joined. This group tried to carry on in the same way as the original community but things were not working. The Vicar and the four ministers together discerned that this new group really needed to go back to the beginning and concentrate on shared stories and sharing lives before beginning to support one another in mission. In the meantime the Vicar, with the support of the four ministers, began a brand new community in one of the other churches in his care.

4

Five years later, about 150 people gathered for a meal in a large hotel to say a formal goodbye to the Vicar, who had been called to move on to another place. They sat at fifteen separate tables, each person with their own small community. The room buzzed with laughter, conversation and Christian fellowship. After a time of worship and the meal a presentation was made to the Vicar. Then he stood up to speak to the gathering.

'I would like to thank you all for coming this evening, and for all you have helped me to learn over the last seven years. When I became Vicar of these four churches, I did not know where to begin. Some of you may remember, I became quite ill in my first year trying to do everything in the old way. As I look back over the last six years it seems to me that little by little the life of our churches has been transformed and that we have found a new way to be church in this place.

'As I look around me this evening I see not four struggling parishes but fifteen small communities of Christian people. These small communities are places where people know one another and are known, where we find friendship, love and support in times of need. They are places where Christian people worship and pray together. They are places of learning and growth. They are communities where everyone is encouraged to use their gifts but also to live out our faith in the whole of our lives: in our workplace, in our family, in the wider society. Each community takes on each year a special mission project to do together as a common task, according to your own discernment of God's call. The time, energy and gifts released for God's mission are far, far greater then ever before in the lives of our parishes.

'When we meet together on Sundays in our buildings for public worship, we come together not just as individuals but as small communities. Six communities meet in one church, four in another, three in another and two in the fourth. As we come together we offer a public witness to the Christian faith in each place and a public invitation to everyone to come and worship and learn and belong. We share together in the ministry of the word and sacrament in a way which enriches and is enriched by the life of our smaller communities. Some of the gifts which have been nurtured in the small groups are now finding an expression in public worship. The mission concerns also are expressed in our prayers of intercession and at special services. Some people come to all of the churches on Sunday who are not part of these smaller communities for various reasons but all share in some of the benefits of belonging to a church in which relationships, faith and mission are supported in this way.

'I would like to express my particular thanks this evening to all those who have given generously of their time and energy to be ministers in these small communities. It has been a joy to work with you, to share what has been happening as you have enabled the life of each group and to discern with you what God is doing in each situation. I thank especially the four people who have shared with me the task of encouraging and supporting the ministers in the groups. You are well skilled in this task now and very able to continue to guide and protect the life of these communities into the future.

'Change is never easy to bring about. The call to change the way that we do church together has not been easy. As you know, there have been problems, mistakes and difficulties along the way. We have needed and still need God's grace and the guidance of God's Spirit. However, we can say with confidence that churches which were stale and tired in their worship and mission have been renewed. We have discovered new and sustainable patterns of fellowship and ministry. We have found ways to grow community in numbers at the same time as growing the bones and structures of that community. We have found ways of enabling mission and the church to grow in numbers and depth as God brings people to us. The change has not been instant or straightforward but it has been deep. I am confident that God will continue what has begun.

'Let me end by reminding you of the place where we began:

'They devoted themselves to the apostles' teaching and fellowship, to the breaking of bread and prayers ... All who believed were together and had all things in common; they would sell their possessions and goods and distribute the proceeds to all, as any had need. Day by day, as they spent much time together in the temple, they broke bread at home and ate their food with glad and generous hearts, praising God and having the goodwill of all the people. And day by day the Lord added to their number those who were being saved.[4]

'"Now I commend you to God and to the message of his grace, a message that is able to build you up and to give you the inheritance among those who are sanctified."'[5]

And all across the room, in and out of the tables, a hundred angels danced the polka and partied into the night.

How far could this be the story of your own church in five years' time?

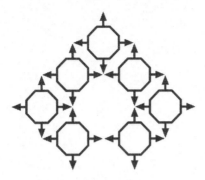

PART TWO

Seeing Clearly: The Church in the Present and the Future

2

Moments of Change

This is an exciting time to be taking up the challenge of ... ministry. We have to re-imagine the Church in the light of Scripture, Tradition and Reason and I am glad to welcome you as a partner in that task ... [1]

Samuel's Story

The prophet Samuel lived in a period of great change for the people of God. As the Book of Judges tells the story, the nation of Israel was a loose confederation of tribes, each with its own territory and leaders. In times of crisis, God raised up a man or woman to unite the nation. These people were called judges. They were given authority over the tribes to call them out to battle against invading enemies and to settle disputes. As time went by, it became clear that this rather loose system of government was no longer working. Israel's enemies grew more powerful. Law, order and common decency began to break down within the community.

Samuel is the last and the greatest of the judges, set aside for God's service from his birth. In his own lifetime, with God's aid, Samuel is able to re-establish a degree of security and order within the nation. The historians describe the settled rhythm of his life in the annual tour he made of the tribes:

> Samuel judged Israel all the days of his life. He went on a circuit year by year to Bethel, Gilgal, and Mizpah; and he judged Israel in all these places. Then he would come back to Ramah for his

home was there; he administered justice there to Israel, and built there an altar to the Lord.[2]

We might imagine that Samuel looked forward to a stable pattern of life and ministry until his retirement or his death. But the elders of Israel have other ideas. Things have been good for the nation under Samuel's leadership but they can see no future beyond his period of office. Samuel's own sons are clearly corrupt, taking bribes and perverting justice. There is no easy way of appointing other leaders to this national position. Tribal jealousies, power struggles and civil war could easily break out. There is a constant threat of invasion and of a return to anarchy where 'all the people did what was right in their own eyes'.[3] In short, the nation has outgrown its old structures of government. The elders come to Samuel, on behalf of the people and demand 'a king to govern us, like other nations'.[4]

At a moment in his life, when he might have been expecting stability, Samuel is therefore caught up in the great movement of cultural change that is affecting his society. In its wider context this change is generated by forces beyond his control. New people groups are moving into Palestine from the Mediterranean. This is creating new pressures on land and therefore renewed armed conflict is inevitable if Israel is to survive. There is a changing technology of war that must be mastered, in particular the development and use of iron weapons.[5] There is now a permanent threat of invasion and conflict such that a nation must be large enough to support a standing army with a warrior-leader who is trained in warfare. There are developments in the potential for trade which only a larger, more united nation can take up. The periods when Israel was without a single leader have led to a decline in faith and morality. There is clearly now a need for continuity and stability. Environmental changes, changing technologies, economic, religious and social changes have built to the extent that they call into question the form of leadership and government in Israel and force a reluctant Samuel to rethink. A completely different way of ordering the life of God's people is required because of forces beyond their control. The world is changing.

Samuel finds this request for change difficult at a number of different levels. Change itself is difficult for most people. Change which involves our own role is doubly so. Accepting that there needs to be change is rarely instant or sudden. Initially, Samuel is badly hurt. It's not only his picture of the future which is called into question but his picture of the past and the present. All my life I've followed this pattern. Have I failed? Have I misunderstood?

There is a vigorous dialogue with God first of all. Does it need to be like this?

> But the thing displeased Samuel when they said, 'Give us a king to govern us.' Samuel prayed to the Lord and the Lord said to Samuel, 'Listen to the voice of the people in all that they say to you; for they have not rejected you, but they have rejected me from being king over them.'[6]

That is followed by a vigorous debate with the people. In a memorable speech, the story-tellers describe through Samuel all the weaknesses of monarchy. But the people persist. A decision is made in favour of change. The new model of government is to be that of kingship 'like the surrounding nations'. Samuel then faces for the rest of his life into his very old age the challenge of leadership in a period of transition. He exchanges his established pattern of ministry – the single task of judging Israel – for three new roles. He must firstly maintain the rhythm of good government in Israel in its previous form, for the present. Otherwise there is the risk of invasion or anarchy. He must secondly, with the people, seek to re-imagine and develop a model of leadership for the people of God which is faithful to their traditions and beliefs but appropriate for the present cultural context. The people have asked for a king to govern us 'like other nations'. The concept of kingship in the surrounding nations has to be refined and challenged within Israel's own traditions (as is happening in 1 Samuel 7). What emerges is, in some ways, a very different model. Thirdly, Samuel must also implement this new style of leadership and government through seeking and appointing a king. These three callings must run together until the new, fledgling institution of the monarchy is able to bear the weight of guiding and guarding the nation. That takes time.

It is a salutary lesson that Samuel's first attempt at appointing a king fails. Saul cannot establish a dynasty (which is one of the main points of the change). It is only with David that a royal house is established and only with Solomon that a mature government emerges. This kind of fundamental change takes time.

Our Story

It doesn't take too much work to draw some parallels between the story of Samuel and the unfolding story of the Church today, especially the older denominations in the Western world. We have evolved and grown used to a way of being church which emerged in a particular time and culture and which worked reasonably well over many generations. It is a way of being church which assumes some or all of the following:

- Christian faith is the default option in society – that people belong to one of the main denominations unless they specifically 'opt out'.
- People meet for worship on Sunday morning in a church which is near to where they live.
- The people in any given congregation on Sundays are a subset of a wider geographical community and therefore already know one another.
- The majority of people in church on Sundays have grown up within the church family.
- Most ministry within the Christian community and outside it is carried out by one or more ordained ministers with some voluntary assistance from the congregation.
- Each church therefore has its own building and a full-time and stipendiary ordained minister who provides the anchor for its life and work.
- The life of each congregation is relatively stable and predictable.

We have inherited this model of being church from those who have gone before us in the faith. In many ways it served them well. Yet we find ourselves living in a period of significant social, economic, technological and cultural change such that this inherited way of being church is no longer working well.[7] Some of these changes have been gradually building for centuries (such as the migration of much of the population from small rural communities to large cities). Some changes are more recent (such as the revolution in knowledge and communication brought about by personal computers and the Internet). However, the cumulative effect of these changes is that the ways of being church which have served reasonably well for generations are either creaking badly or are no longer working.

Some of the key changes which challenge the way we are church together are:[8]

- Christian faith is no longer the 'default option' for the majority in our society. The proportion of those who consider themselves to be Christian in any real sense declines each year. For most of those who are under thirty and many over that age, Christianity is something to be chosen or opted into rather than an assumed faith.[9]
- We are now much more conscious of living in a multi-cultural and multi-faith society. Almost everyone in Great Britain is aware that Christianity is one world faith among several. For anyone from a secular background considering faith, Christianity is one option. A large section of society is now affected in one way or another with approaches to religion and spirituality which are grouped under the loose heading of 'New Age'.
- There is considerable evidence that our society has undergone a significant change in the way in which people think. This change is often described as a move to a post-modern society. One Christian author summarises the change like this:

> Postmodernism says goodbye to big stories or metanarratives that are grand explanations of the truth (Enlightenment), history (Marxism) or faith (Christianity). In their place are a multitude of local stories, often conflicting, but celebrating their illogicality and diversity. This fragmentation applies to our cultural, social and religious realms where the consumer reigns. Everything becomes an item for consumption: education, health care, knowledge and religion make consumers of parents and children, patients, students and worshippers ... The confident culture of modernism, optimistic, utopian and progressive, has been replaced with a diffident, often hope-less and anxious spirit about our age.[10]

- Society is more mobile in every sense. People are more ready to move house and area than we were a generation ago.[11] Car ownership is much higher. As a society we travel significant distances for work, leisure and shopping. There is evidence to suggest that people are also prepared to travel greater distances to attend church either because of preference for a particular style of worship or because they have moved out of an area but wish to keep a link with the faith community there.

- In many parts of the country, congregations are therefore no longer subgroups of communities which exist outside the local church. People no longer work, play, shop or worship in the area in which they live. Apart from parents at home with young children, or the elderly, there are few natural networks based upon geography. Churches have therefore become 'primary communities' – places where people meet and get to know one another for the first time (and potentially very important building blocks for relationships in our wider society).

- The pattern of Sunday has changed for many people over the last decade with the relaxation of the laws on Sunday trading. A higher proportion of people now work on Sundays.[12] Organisations which support work with children testify that the higher incidence of marriage breakdown means that young people are often dividing their weekends between two family homes.[13]

- These developments together with changes in the way people use their leisure time and increased demands from the workplace for many means that, in general, more people in our society attend church less often. Studies of congregation attendance patterns in 1999 in the Dioceses of Wakefield and Ripon (as it then was) demonstrated that a normal Sunday attendance figure of 60 adults no longer represents 60 people coming to church each week but may represent 120 people, 30 of whom worship weekly, 30 come to worship once a fortnight and 60 of whom attend once a month. These proportions, of course, vary significantly from place to place. In turn this pattern means that the Sunday congregation is never the same for two weeks running. When combined with the increased likelihood that the person leading the service will be different from week to week (explored in the next section) this means a major adjustment is needed in the way we think about communication and community building in Christian congregations: new ways of belonging and defining community are needed.[14] There is evidence that it is becoming much harder to find those who will be committed to working with children and young people on a weekly basis on Sundays.[15]

- Although there are many congregations where the majority have grown up within the Christian family, there are also many where a large proportion of the adult church members have become Christians and/or joined that particular church in adult life. Research undertaken in the Church of England Diocese of Lichfield in 1999 indicated that 61 per cent of parishes were running some sort of process-evangelism course. Over 6,000 people had attended courses across the diocese and of these, 22 per cent had come to Christian faith, commitment or confirmation during the courses. There is anecdotal evidence to suggest that this pattern is repeated across many Anglican dioceses.[16] Spiritual, emotional, learning and community needs and expectations are often very different. The Church as a whole understands much more about how adults come to faith at the end of the decade of evangelism than we did at the beginning. Running effective groups for enquirers and new Christians is possible for any congregation and most will see some fruit from their work.
- There has been a very significant development in lay ministry of every kind both outside of and within congregations. This recovery of the ministry of the whole people of God has been very well grounded theologically and has had an enormous and positive impact on the lives of many individual Christians and on churches.[17]
- All of this means that the life of many congregations is anything but static and predictable. Either change is initiated from within or unwelcome change is pressed upon a reluctant community externally through pastoral re-organisation or other changes.

What is the effect of all of this change on the life of the churches? There is no simple picture either of overall decline or overall growth. The 'net' figure of overall Sunday attendance or membership (however that is measured) for a circuit, deanery, diocese, district or denomination is made up of a large number of figures for individual congregations, each of which shows its own pattern of growth or decline. A group of ten churches may show an overall decline of 5 per cent in normal Sunday attendance over a five-year period. But when you look more closely, you may find that two churches in that circuit or deanery have actually seen significant and sustained growth; four others have been in very steep decline and one has closed; three have stayed about the same.

The way this pattern is worked out varies significantly both across regions and between denominations and church traditions:

- Sunday attendance for all denominations declined by 33 per cent in Yorkshire and Humberside over the ten years from 1989 to 1998. In the same period the decline was only 5 per cent in Greater London.[18]
- Roman Catholic attendance at Mass over the ten years declined by 28 per cent. The Methodist rate of decline was similar at 26 per cent. However, over the same ten-year period, in the same cultural conditions, the Baptist Church grew by 2 per cent and the New Churches increased by 38 per cent.[19]
- According to Brierley's analysis, churches describing themselves as evangelical have declined by just 3 per cent; churches describing themselves as catholic by 48 per cent.[20]

The differences are very significant and are reflected in the anecdotal evidence: almost any edition of a church newspaper will contain both stories reflecting growth ('Church seeks larger premises/Record numbers on Alpha Courses') and those reflecting decline ('Diocese to cut 25 posts').[21]

Numbers cannot measure everything (as we shall certainly see in later chapters). However, at the very least the statistics show us that individual congregations are responding in very different ways to the changes affecting us all. The evidence suggests that some churches are able to change, adapt and flourish but others do not. It is not the case at all, therefore, that the wider changes in Church and society mean *inevitable* decline.[22] Several recent cultural changes may actually mean a more favourable climate for the spread of the gospel. But the evidence does indicate that, if it is to develop and flourish, the Church must adapt and change within its new context and environment. This need to change is not a new thing. Throughout the two thousand years of Christian history, and as the gospel has spread from place to place and from culture to culture, the Church has needed to reflect upon every aspect of its life, to change, develop and adapt. That challenge is with us now in a particularly acute form.

Clergy and Congregations

There is, however, one further change we need to highlight which is profoundly affecting the growth or development of church life at the present time and that is the ratio of stipendiary clergy to congregations and the relationship between the two. As we have seen, the inherited model of being church holds as its normal assumption that each congregation will have its own stipendiary minister who will undertake much of the ministry both within and on behalf of the Christian community. Over the past twenty years we have seen (and are seeing) a very significant change in this established pattern.

The reasons for this decline in the ratio of clergy to congregations are complex and vary from denomination to denomination. In the Roman Catholic Church, there has been a significant downturn in the number of vocations to the priesthood over the past twenty-five years which is now having a serious effect on the life of parishes.[23] In the Church of England and the Methodist Church vocations to stipendiary ministry are on the increase at present. The decline in the number of clergy is in part connected with their age profile: more are due to retire over the next five years than are due to be ordained. This in turn is connected with the fact that more clergy have been ordained in later life over the past thirty years. The decline in the number of posts which can be supported by dioceses and districts is also closely connected with a number of significant economic changes. It is only within the last thirty-five years that the Church of England has made adequate provision for its clergy to retire (in step with thinking about retirement in our wider society) both through housing provision and pensions. The cost of this provision has, of course risen, both with inflation and as the numbers of retired clergy grows year by year as the average life expectancy increases. At the same time, the value of the Church of England's historic resources has fallen in real terms. The expectations of the clergy in terms of housing, stipend and expenses have probably also risen in the same period (although this is harder to measure). The outcome is that parishes in the Church of England have had to shoulder the burden for the whole of clergy stipends and housing provision and an increasing share of the pension contributions. It is very hard to convince parishes that giving to the diocese should be increased at the same time as the numbers of clergy are being reduced. The dangers of some Anglican dioceses slipping into a rapid spiral of decline seem very real at the present time.

But what are the consequences of the amalgamation of parishes for the life of the Church and for the life of the clergy? We will explore this in greater detail in the next chapter. Two are worth highlighting at this point. The first is the effect on the time and energy of the stipendiary clergy. A higher proportion of energy and time is demanded by routine administration (surprisingly high in parish ministry), arranging and leading worship (even where others are involved) and servicing church meetings. In urban areas, a significant increase in the population served by the larger parish will also normally mean an increase in the number of occasional offices, particularly the taking of funerals. This increased workload is likely to mean a reduction in the time and energy available for work in two other key areas: service in the wider community (in schools, development projects and the like) and the development of the life and mission of the churches. Many clergy will derive a significant part of their motivation and satisfaction from one or both of these areas of work. Reducing the time spent on these things may therefore, in turn, lead to a loss of motivation and morale. Bishop Michael Turnbull has articulated recently the widespread sense throughout the Church that this process cannot continue:

> But bolting parishes together cannot go on without taking a look at the consequences. This policy has had a severe effect on the working patterns of clergy – probably to the detriment of pastoral care and evangelism – since clergy time is taken up with leading too many services, a huge burden of occasional offices without the time to use the teaching opportunities they offer, looking after several buildings and supervising duplicated electoral and administrative structures. Such arrangements have had consequences for the health and morale of clergy and active lay people, all of whom are ministering in an increasingly secular context, the consequent reduction of congregational numbers and an effect on active lay participation and financial support. We cannot continue on that road as ministry in an alien situation will overwork

and oppress the clergy, especially when they are working in isolation and running hard, at best, to stand still.[24]

In addition to factors of time and energy, there is a parallel change in congregational expectations and a shift in the dynamics of power which are created by the new arrangements: 'The changes in the financing of Church of England parishes since the 1980s have led to a profound cultural shift in parochial and ministerial self-understanding. Increasingly, it is the congregations who are now paying directly for "their" parish priests and, correspondingly, they are becoming more demanding of their ministers.'[25] Congregations which are being asked to contribute more towards the provision of ministers might reasonably expect (one would think) a somewhat 'better service' – at the very least that the stipendiary minister would spend more time with members of the congregation than the wider community.

Church and Ministry

Within the Church of England at the present time (and to a certain extent within other denominations) there is an attempt to respond to this fundamental change in the pattern of church life by a great deal of systematic reflection upon Christian ministry.[26] New patterns of ministry have been developed (such as ordained local ministry and recognised lay pastoral ministers); new ways of collaborative working are commended both within and across churches; there has been systematic reflection upon the changing role of stipendiary ministers and what is needed for their initial and continuing training. Much of this thinking has been well earthed in theology as well as practical considerations and the Church of England's Director of Ministry was able to report at the end of 2001 a well thought through consensus emerging.[27] So far so good. Yet this new and creative thinking about ministry will only take us so far unless there is also new and creative thinking about the way in which we are church. Much of the new thinking about collaborative ministry assumes (or can be understood to assume) that the church can and should continue in its present form and way of operating. Therefore the priority in ministry strategy must be to provide the necessary ministers to enable that to happen. If there is a shortfall in the number of stipendiary clergy then we need more part-time and voluntary ministers, both lay and ordained. Hence the massive effort in this direction at the present time.

But suppose for a moment that it is the present way in which we are being church that is not working? If that is the case, then no amount of new thinking about ministry in isolation will be enough to take us forward. We may find ourselves working harder and harder to achieve less and less. It is the contention of this book that a new vision of what it means to be church is required, not simply new thinking about ministry.[28]

A Time of Transition

As in the time of Samuel, so in the present day: the old ways which have served us the people of God well are no longer working. Change is needed. This in turn means that those called to guide and guard the life of the Christian community in the present day have, like Samuel, three tasks:

1. In the words of the Bishop of London quoted at the head of this chapter, 'we have to re-imagine the Church in the light of Scripture, Tradition and Reason'. A new vision is needed not simply for ordained ministry or even for collaborative ministry but for the whole life of the Church.
2. We must maintain and care for what is good in the established way of being church, recognising that there is much that is good and some people and congregations who are simply unable to change.
3. At the same time we are called with time and patience to bring about change for the future shape of the local church in accordance with the re-imagining and fresh vision.

The whole of this task will be the work of the present generation of Christian ministers. Lay and ordained Christian ministers are therefore called to a dual vocation which might be described as transitional leadership: to care for what is yet also to seek out and bring into being something new. What that 'something new' might be is the subject of this book.

Do you agree with this analysis of where we are at present?

How far can you identify with the vocation to transitional leadership?

3

Renewing
Vision

Josiah and the Scroll

How does new vision emerge? The story of Josiah has something to teach us. The story-tellers who collected and edited the Old Testament accounts of the kings of Judah see the reign of Josiah as one of the few moments of light in a long history of decline. Josiah began his reign in 640 BC when he was eight years old, following the assassination of his father, Amon. His grandfather, Manasseh, had previously reigned for fifty-five years and that reign is regarded by the historians as the low point for the kings of Judah in terms of religious apostasy, immorality and the shedding of innocent blood.[1] Eighteen years into Josiah's reign, the Book of Kings describes the finding of a certain book of the law within the temple. The way the story is told, it is as if the scroll is brought to light during the extensive repair work being undertaken in the sanctuary.

The scroll is discovered by the high priest and passed to Shaphan, the secretary, who in turn delivers it to the king.[2] When it is read to Josiah, the words have a remarkable effect: 'When the king heard the words of the book of the law, he tore his clothes.' Guidance is sought from a prophet, Huldah the wife of Shallum. She confirms that the words are indeed from God, although they are long forgotten, and still apply to the nation of Josiah's day. In the ancient words of the scroll Josiah finds the inspiration he needs in his generation to bring about renewal and change for the nation. Many commentators have thought that the rediscovered book of the law contains all or part of the present book of Deuteronomy. Whatever its precise content, the book of the covenant is read in the hearing of all the people and the covenant itself is renewed:

The king stood by the pillar and made a covenant before the Lord, to follow the Lord, keeping his commandments, his decrees, and his statutes, with all his heart and all his soul, to perform the words of this covenant that were written in this book. All the people joined in the covenant.[3]

In the years that follow, there is change. A new vision has emerged. A programme began to centralise, simplify and renew the worshipping life of Israel, following the guidance given in the scroll. The temple was cleansed of all the items used in the worship of other gods. Alternative places of worship were destroyed. At the end of this period of purification, as the people were recalled to the worship of God, Josiah celebrated the Passover: 'No such passover had been kept since the days of the judges who judged Israel, and during all the days of the kings of Israel or of the kings of Judah'.[4]

Although the efforts made in the time of Josiah are not enough to save Judah from destruction, undoubtedly the reformation played a key role in laying the foundation for the life of God's people in exile and beyond. Something vital was recovered. The law was taught to the whole people. A school of theology and understanding developed which was to shape a large part of what we know today as the Old Testament and the later life of Judaism.

What was the source of this renewed vision for the life of the people of God? The story suggests that Josiah and his associates are holding in tension two elements: the book of the law, on the one hand, with its description of how things can and should be for the nation, and their present experience of life in Judah, on the other hand, which is very different: worship, and therefore priorities are confused. Fresh vision and energy for renewal come from holding these two elements together (the book and the reality) and seeing the gap, the distance between them. Experience and observation of the context alone are not enough. Being immersed in the book of the law alone is insufficient. Where the book of the law and the signs of the times are combined, the result is a movement of renewal which affects a generation.

Before we leave the story, it is worth reflecting on what the writers mean us to understand by the mysterious discovery of the book of the law at this particular moment in Israel's history. The story is careful not to ascribe it to divine providence or to an accidental discovery. The implication is that the book of the law has been in the temple for the whole time, waiting to be discovered by those who went looking in the right places. In the same way, the story suggests, God's people always have access to resources which might describe, define and inspire a better way.

Looking for New Vision

We acknowledge that change is needed but where do we gain the vision that will give us new direction? There is a widespread recognition that some kind of transformation is required in the way we are church. However, as we will see in the following chapter, most of the current approaches seek to draw inspiration and direction largely from the prevailing context, in slightly different ways. The cinema model looks at the problem in terms of managing changing resources for ministry; the franchise model attempts to reproduce what works in different places. Those who see the church as a unit of production focus on how to do one task really well through a local congregation, hoping that the making of new disciples will itself generate renewed vision. The quality control model develops tools to answer the question: to what kind of church do we most want to belong? The fifth model seeks to take its inspiration for how to be church entirely from the shifting patterns in our culture.

It is unlikely that any of these approaches will produce new and lasting vision for the church in the twenty-first century by themselves, although elements from each may be needed. To re-imagine the church for a new context we need, like Josiah, to be immersed in and familiar with our context. Yet we also need our equivalent of the book of the law. Our understanding of what the church is called to be and meant to be is impoverished and needs to be fed, nurtured and developed. It is from these two elements that new vision will be forged.

A great deal has been written in recent years about the (sometimes) elusive concept of vision for individual lives, churches and other organisations.[5] Most writers are agreed on its importance: a clear vision of the future is essential to the development of any endeavour. A strong vision has the capacity to energise all involved in the organisation towards the same goals. Where there is a common vision there is the potential for teamwork; the continuous involvement of new people; effective sharing of tasks and responsibilities; sacrificing short-term gains for the long-term view and a common reference point for resolving conflict. Where there is no coherent vision in a church context, ministry is likely to be reactive and short term in its focus. There will be conflicts of expectation and direction and little momentum for change. Co-operative work will be difficult. It is likely to be hard to involve new people and those who are involved are likely to be low in motivation and morale and liable to disengage from what is happening. The development, discernment and articulation of vision is therefore increasingly seen as an essential task of leadership in all contexts.

The literature is less clear, however, on the ways in which that vision develops. Even secular writers can portray the process in mystical language: vision for the future somehow emerges. It is part of an indefinable charism given to leaders that they are able to see a different future. In fact, the process is best seen as a very simple one. As in the story of Josiah, vision emerges when we compare reality with an ideal. As we become more and more aware of the gap between the two pictures, so there is an impetus for change and development.

In order to develop fresh vision for the church, therefore, or for any aspect of Christian ministry, the following elements must be part of the process.

1. Listen to the context

In the case of a small group of people wrestling to gain fresh vision for a group of local churches, this will mean getting to know the history of the congregations; the different ways of belonging; the stories of the individual people. Normally this will be through a combination of simply listening to a wide range of people reflect on the situation and tell their story and the use of various research tools such as local histories, statistical analysis of church records, census information, mission audit of the local community,[6] congregational questionnaires to measure people's experience of church life; and so on. Listening in this way requires honesty, humility and courage to face weaknesses as well as strengths in order to make space for new ideas to emerge and to face the possibilities of change.

In all of this listening, attention must be paid to the general trends in society but also to the particular story of a given congregation. As an illustration of this, I have pondered for many years a passage I discovered in a little booklet produced in 1923 to tell the story of the establishing of St George's, Ovenden, the parish where I was vicar from 1987 to 1996. The church was founded in 1877 through the generosity of a local benefactor, Miss Moss, daughter of the vicar of the neighbouring parish of Illingworth. The first incumbent, Israel Parkinson, was curate of that parish and a man of remarkable gifts and energy. Mr Parkinson remained as vicar until 1909, when he retired on health grounds and the period of ministry was extraordinarily fruitful. Measured in terms of buildings alone, the parishioners (who were not wealthy by any means) built a Sunday School in 1879, which soon attracted 400 scholars, a vicarage in 1883 and re-opened a mission church in 1889. In 1911, Mr Parkinson looked back on that extraordinary period of activity and the reasons for it.

> He thought that besides what [Miss Moss] provided, there was a second blessing in what she did not provide. Miss Moss sent for him and she said: 'Mr. Parkinson, I am very anxious to avoid at St. George's, the mistake into which my good friend Colonel Ackroyd fell when he built All Souls' and so overwhelmed them with gifts that, for a time, there will no doubt be almost a state of paralysis upon them, when he is no longer able to support them'. She left them to help themselves, so that, at the consecration of the Church, there was no bell with which to summon the congregation to prayer, there was no congregation belonging to the Church if there had been a bell. There was no house for him or his successors to enjoy the comforts of life, there was no school, no parish, no endowment whatever, to support the minister and year passed into year before that came to the parish. But notice the result. It called every one of us to show what mettle there was in us. I remember meeting the first vicar of All Soul's one day and he said, 'I do envy you Mr.

Parkinson'. 'Why, Mr. Holmes?' He replied, 'Because you, at St. George's, whatever you put your hand to, you can accomplish it.'[7]

When I first arrived in the parish, I met one man in his late eighties who had been baptised by Mr Parkinson. There was continuity over the course of a century not just in the families connected to the church but in the spirit. My predecessor, Chris Edmondson, and myself, were vicars of St George's through a time when a great deal of work was needed on the buildings: over a ten-year period a new hall was built, the church repaired and re-ordered, and the old vicarage purchased from the diocese and converted to a parish centre. Almost all the resources came from within the congregation in money, expertise and time. It was always thought provoking, in the light of Mr Parkinson's words, to look across the valley to see the spire of All Souls' Church where the building had been declared redundant in the 1970s and the congregation had sadly dwindled to a couple of dozen: neighbouring churches in similar places on the socio-economic scale, travelling through the same cultural changes, but with a very different story and character. At least part of the difference lay in the foundations laid over a hundred years ago.

2. Nurture your picture of what is possible

In order to develop vision which is genuinely new, there needs to be a similar investment in thinking creatively about how things can be different. In a secular enterprise this may mean looking at a range of different materials (including similar organisations in different contexts) and engaging in imaginative 'possibility thinking'. *The Complete Idiot's Guide to Leadership* has a list of sources of information in a box headed 'How to Create Vision in a Hurry':

> To form a vision you have to look beyond the immediate future to create an image of what the organization or unit is capable of becoming. A vision highlights the discrepancy between the present and ideal conditions and provides people with something to strive towards ... Here are some sources of information for creating a vision, thus jump-starting you as a high impact leader:

1. Your own imagination about future possibilities
2. Your own intuition about developments in your field, the markets you serve and the preferences of your constituents
3. The work of futurists as it relates to your kind of work
4. Group discussions about what it would take to please the people your group serves
5. Annual reports and management books that describe the vision statements being formulated by others
6. Speaking to group members individually and collectively to learn about their hopes and dreams for the future
7. For an organizational unit, studying the entire organisation's vision and developing one that is compatible.[8]

For a church or group of churches this may be a useful guide for part of the process but on its own it is simply not enough. An essential part of developing vision is nourishing our often impoverished ideas of what it means to be the Christian community, the people of God. This happens through study, reflection and learning together and also through experiencing different ways of being church. The raw materials for that study will be the Scriptures and the Christian tradition, the story of how Christians have thought about their common life over two thousand years and in many different contexts.

It is this step of the process which is all too often omitted in reflection about the future shape of church and ministry and it is largely for this reason that our future vision is both greatly impoverished and open to a theological critique. We move directly from observation of our context to a solution without, as it were, going past 'Go' and collecting the other resources we need for development. A vision built on an emaciated theology of what it means to be church will not satisfy and provides an inadequate foundation for the building of a healthy church.

Where both of these stages are happening in parallel, over time a number of ideas will begin to emerge in the space between the ideal and the reality. As these ideas begin to coalesce, it is in this space that a renewed vision emerges.

Listen to the Context

⇩

Vision is found in the gap

⇧

Nurture the Picture

3. Discern your vocation

At this point in the development of vision in a secular community, a group may typically have brainstormed about a number of different possibilities. Not all will be possible in terms of the resources available. Some may be inappropriate for the organisation or impractical. Some may be mutually conflicting. The third part of the task is to sift these possibilities until the most likely options emerge so that these can be further refined and tested.

There is an additional dimension, however, in discerning vision for any Christian community and particularly for a church, and that is the discernment of vocation. There will be a large number of disparities between the life of the church in reality and the vision of what it could be. These may involve areas for significant development (such as lay ministry) or areas for significant mission (to asylum seekers in the community). Not all of these areas will be possible in terms of the resources available. Some may be inappropriate or impractical. Some may be mutually conflicting. The discernment of which ways forward are the right ones is a matter for prayer and listening to God as much as it is a matter for discussion and decision making.

Once again, this is a part of the process which does not receive due attention. Following the publication of the *Faith in the City* Report in

1983, many dioceses in the Church of England produced and used material for mission audit. The material was (and continues to be) an excellent tool for helping any congregation examine its local community. However, the assumption in the material was that it was possible to move directly from identifying a pressing need in the community (a large number of unemployed people) to the Christian congregation meeting that need without either costing the endeavour in terms of resources or reflecting before God on questions of priorities and vocation.

4. Ask: 'What kind of vision are we seeking?'

Something strange has happened to the word 'vision' in our contemporary society. At its root is a rich theological seam, present throughout Scripture, concerned with 'seeing clearly' and seeing as God sees in terms of both the present and the future. Such vision is recognised as difficult to attain and as a gift from God: think of the story of Balaam, Elisha's servant, Jesus' teaching about the parables, Simon Peter's declaration about the Messiah or the disciples on the road to Emmaus.[9] Vision in Scripture can be as much about the present as the future.

In the modern world, this term 'vision', with all its depth of meaning, has been borrowed from the language of theology by the language first of politics then of business and management. As it has come to be used by the latter, the word has, understandably, attracted a much simpler meaning: that of a plan or picture of the future for a business, charity or organisation.[10] Because the term is used primarily in a commercial or secular framework, 'vision' is more closely connected to an imagined future and linked to the concepts of continuous growth and increased revenue.[11] Vision was once the preserve of *prophets*. It now has more to do with the generation of *profits*.

As the church has recognised the need to adapt to a changing world, Christians have begun to use the term 'vision' again for the recasting of an imagined future for the church. The word 'vision' is one which sits very comfortably, of course, in the Christian vocabulary. However, much of the time when the word is used, the meaning seems now to be taken from the business world not the Christian tradition. It has come to mean, therefore, for the churches, an imagined future which, nine times out of ten, has to do with a future picture of the continual growth and influence of a particular local community or denomination.

The term 'vision' is not the only piece of theological language to be used by the business community and therefore to be subject to this devaluation through being borrowed and borrowed back. 'Mission' has been treated in a similar way. The terms 'charismatic', 'steward', 'servant', 'community' and 'transformation' are all found in the secular leadership texts.[12] It is the term 'vision', however, which has lost the most in the translation and whose biblical content and meaning needs to be recovered by the churches as we re-imagine what it means to be church. The danger is that we reduce the calling to be the people of God to the kind of vision which is appropriate for a commercial company, with all that this implies. In thinking about the process of developing fresh vision, it is therefore important to ask what may make a Christian vision for the church different from a vision for any other organisation and to repossess some of the content of the biblical concept. Some of this material will be explored in more detail in Part Four of the book. However, it is important to note the following points here:

Horizons
In the commercial world, the vision generated is normally simply for the benefit of the organisation and its shareholders or employees. For the church, the vision must be for the benefit and blessing of the whole world, not simply for the Christian community or any particular part of it. Our horizon must be on the kingdom of God rather than the extension of influence of a congregation or denomination.

God's vision
In the world of business, organisations attempt to generate and discover their own vision and plan for the future. The responsibility of the church is not simply to generate ideas (although there is a place for human creativity) nor to invent something but discover the vision which God has for the Church as a whole and for a particular local congregation. That vision will be a mixture of what we are called to be and what we are called to do. We might think of the picture of the risen Christ tending the seven lampstands in Revelation 1, or of the story of the Exodus: God guides his people not only in

the general particulars of the journey but also the specifics through a pillar of cloud by day and a pillar of fire by night.[13]

Looking below the surface

In the world of business organisations, the emphasis is understandably upon what is measurable (profitability; number of patients treated, numbers of students enrolled). In the biblical tradition of vision, there is a parallel emphasis on what is unseen and immeasurable. Numbers have some value, especially where they represent people, although there is certainly a tradition in Scripture which warns of the danger of being deceived by them.[14] However, the hidden qualities and virtues in a person or a nation are prized more highly than public appearance or success.[15] What is outwardly successful may be inwardly impoverished. Travelling well is more important than arriving first. Well attended and effective worship services mean little without right conduct: 'Take away from me the noise of your songs; I will not listen to the melody of your harps. But let justice roll down like waters and righteousness like an ever-flowing stream.'[16]

The perspective of the gospel

Vision in business and organisations is likely to be about protecting their own interests and extending their own influence: saving their life and gaining the world. Jesus says to his disciples (individually and corporately):

> 'If any want to become my followers, let them deny themselves and take up their cross and follow me. For those who want to save their life will lose it, and those who lose their life for my sake will find it. For what will it profit them if they gain the whole world but forfeit their life? Or what will they give in return for their life?'[17]

The heart of the Christian gospel is the death and resurrection of Jesus. At the centre of our Christian faith is the message of the Son of God giving up his life and being raised up when it seemed all had failed. That is also to be the pattern for the church. A vision which says we must die in order to live and invest ourselves in that which is unlikely to yield any obvious return is a different kind of vision from the normal business model but is closer to the pattern and priorities of Christ. The perspective of the gospel also yields the truth that the barren can give birth, the wasteland can become a fruitful garden and what is dead can rise to new life. In the economy of God, we should expect the unexpected. Neat graphs about future trends (whether positive or negative) are unlikely to be realised. The weak are to be nurtured back to life, not discarded: '... a bruised reed he will not break, and a dimly burning wick he will not quench ...'[18]

Achieving the right approach to the possibility of fruitful ministry is vital for individuals and the churches. There are large sections of the Church which are so influenced by cynicism and failure that they find it difficult to accept that churches and Christian ministry can ever be fruitful and effective. Yet there are other sections of the Church which will happily swallow the camel that continual growth and success is a necessary part of proclaiming the gospel and validates whatever methods are used. The truth lies somewhere between the two.

The rhythm of growth

The models of vision taken from the commercial world operate largely on the hypothesis that continuous growth and development is possible for any organisation. I suspect the idea of continuous growth is a mythical ideal even in the world of economics and organisations. It certainly does not transfer easily either to individuals or to human communities such as churches. Growth in a person is more likely to come in periods of crisis or change than to be spread evenly over the course of a lifetime. The story of the Exodus is not a story of even progress towards a goal but a kind of three steps forward, two steps back type of journey in which the detours can be as important as direct movement towards the goal and the overall feel can be one of going round in circles (which is much more like the experience of many churches). We need to question the idea that individuals and communities can sustain continual meaningful growth over long periods of time: the experience is likely to lead to overextension, burnout, retreat and exhaustion as it is to real progress. We are human beings! We need times for rest and reflection as well as times of focused action: green pastures and still waters as well as steep and rugged pathways.[19] Churches, like people and vines,[20] need seasons of rest and renewal as well as seasons of growth.

41

5. Test, weigh and refine the vision

Different Christian communities will evolve different ways of generating new vision which in most cases will be a combination of individual gifts and small group activity. Unless the congregation is very small, it will normally be impossible for the whole group to go through the entire process together. However, there will come a point where, having generated some provisional ideas, these need to be tested and weighed by the whole community, or all who can and will share in the process. This is not the moment to declare 'This is our vision for the future', like Moses coming down from the mountaintop. It is rather the moment to say: 'You agreed that a group of us should do some reflection on what we are called to be and to become as a church now and in the future. We've done our best with that task. So far it's involved looking at our society and community and the story of our church. It's meant Bible study and discussion together as we have tried to develop our understanding of what it means to be church. We initially came up with a lot of ideas and now we've refined those down to the ones which seem to us to be the most important. But now we want to know what you think. How does this seem to you?'

The account of the Council of Jerusalem in Acts 15 can be read as a story of the early Church testing and weighing two different visions and possibilities for the future. Was the Church called to be a predominantly Jewish community, to which Gentiles could belong but only if they accepted the Jewish law and customs? Or was the vision a much greater one to build a Church which was inclusive of Gentiles whether or not they abided by this law?[21] There is debate over several days, no doubt in the context of worship and prayer. In the end the apostles and elders are able to say on behalf of the whole community: 'it has seemed good to the Holy Spirit and to us to impose on you no further burden than these essentials ...'[22]

In order to test a vision for the future of the church, of course, the whole community must be involved to some degree in learning about their own context and developing their understanding of what it means to be church. The process is therefore about learning together as much as it is about making decisions.[23]

6. Communicate clearly

The secular texts place an enormous emphasis on the clear, consistent and imaginative communication of a common vision.[24] Here, at least, is one instance where secular wisdom and the Scriptures are in complete agreement. Those who are most associated with vision in the Scriptures, the prophets, are exceptional communicators. The very word 'prophet' means one who speaks. Among their tools of communication are powerful preaching, vivid images, the use of their own experiences, prophetic actions, parables and stories, humour, dialogue and rebuke, written messages, drama and mime, and incarnating the message into their own life. Passion and emotion are an essential part of enabling people to see. The act of communicating vision is far more than rehearsing a neat statement or going through a list of bullet points. The thought of Ezekiel using an overhead projector and a list to get across his message is a strange one.[25]

At the very heart of the communication of vision is helping people to see clearly. The reasons why we cannot see are complex, as many of the gospel stories reveal. The causes of blindness include pride, prejudice, greed, self-interest, guilt and fear as well as ignorance. Blindness afflicts communities as well as individuals. Jesus' parables are developed in part to expose exactly this kind of blindness in order that we can see. The classic example is the story of the good Samaritan, which helps all those who enter into the story to glimpse both their own prejudice and gain a much broader vision of what it means to love your neighbour as yourself.

The communication of vision about the church to the church, therefore, is not some secondary level activity, peripheral to the main task: it is at the heart of the enterprise and demands our best gifts and energies. The education of the whole church into what it means to be the church is an essential part of our common life.

Seeking New Vision

Josiah discovers a scroll when he is not looking for anything in particular. The Church today consciously needs to seek fresh vision about the renewal of its life, particularly at local level. That vision will come only as we grow in our understanding both of our present context and of what the church is called to be. In the emerging gap between the ideal and the reality new and good things will grow. These need to be tested, refined, owned, communicated and acted upon at local level. The rest of what follows is an attempt to sketch a picture for the whole Church and to provide resources for this broader task.

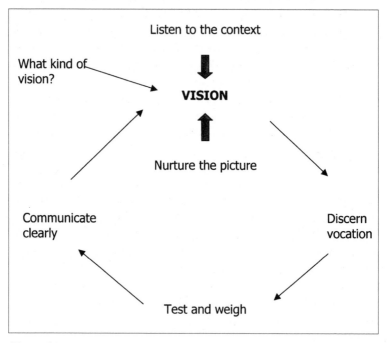

Figure 1.

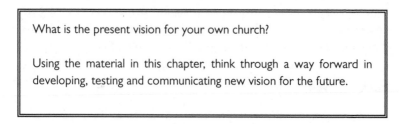

4

Models for
the Future?

Rehoboam and the Tribes of Israel

The first Book of Kings recounts the story of Rehoboam's choice at
the beginning of his reign. Rehoboam is Solomon's successor and
heir to the extensive and united kingdom which holds together all
twelve tribes of Israel. At the beginning of his reign, representatives
of the tribes gather together at Shechem, in a scene similar to the
encounter between Samuel and the people described in the previous
chapter. The elders of the people demand a lighter load. The burdens
of kingship have become too great, rather as Samuel predicted. The
people say to the new king: 'Your father made our yoke heavy. Now
therefore lighten the hard service of your father and his heavy yoke
that he placed on us, and we will serve you.'[1] Rehoboam asks for
three days to reflect on his answer. In that time, he takes counsel
with two groups: the first are the older men who were Solomon's
advisers. They reply in words which are worth remembering and
repeating to anyone who is beginning new responsibilities and
work, whether inside or outside the Church: 'If you will be a servant
to this people today and serve them and speak good words to them
when you answer them, then they will be your servants for ever.'[2]
The foundation of authority is to become a servant.[3] The beginning
of a relationship in which a person or group is entrusted with
influence must be to listen to what that group is saying. Mutual
accountability is a necessary part of building a relationship of trust.
Once that relationship of trust is established, it can bear the weight

of leadership, influence and change. At the beginning it is a fragile plant and needs to be nurtured. There are lessons here for all kinds of ministry and ministry teams.

These lessons are reinforced by the way in which the account continues. Rehoboam also seeks advice from his contemporaries who, perhaps, belong to a generation which need to prove themselves. They answer him in a different way:

> 'Thus you should say to this people who spoke to you. "Your father made our yoke heavy, but you must lighten it for us"; thus you should say to them, "My little finger is thicker than my father's loins. Now, whereas my father laid on you a heavy yoke, I will add to your yoke. My father disciplined you with whips, but I will discipline you with scorpions."'[4]

The advice is the opposite of that given by Solomon's counsellors: assertive where the older advisers step back; arrogant rather than humble; aggressive instead of conciliatory; crude rather than courteous and respectful.

Questions are being asked here not only of Rehoboam's policy but also about his character. Is he able to listen? Can the new king see what needs changing after Solomon's long reign? Is he secure enough in himself to allow some power to pass back to the people? The king is being tested right at the beginning of his reign. Will he pass the test or will he be found wanting?

From Rehoboam's perspective, the choice is a real one and will have significant consequences for the future (although not the ones he foresees). It appears from the story that his character is already formed (something which itself has lessons for the training of those entrusted with responsibility). The answer the king gives is that offered by the younger men. The key mistake he makes is that he 'did not listen to the people' (v. 15). The effects of his decision are, in this instance, immediate, catastrophic and long lasting. Ten of the twelve tribes of Israel secede from Rehoboam. His rival, Jeroboam, establishes a larger and more powerful northern kingdom with its capital at Samaria and its own centres of worship. There is civil war between the two countries. The united nation ceases to be a significant power in the region and becomes instead two small, squabbling kingdoms. Eventually both will be overcome by foreign powers invading from the north. Never again will the whole nation be re-united under a single ruler. The seeds of the destruction of the monarchy have been sown.

In our own generation, as we have seen, the Church at every level faces choices about her future. We need to discover new directions. It is likely that there will be a range of different advice offered, not all of it compatible. After a period of reflection, decisions will need to be made (even if those decisions are to do nothing). Those choices and decisions will have their consequences for individual congregations, for denominations and for the communities in which they are set. Some roads may prove fruitful. Others may lead to difficulty or even disaster. Investing time in listening to a range of counsel and weighing it carefully is vital.

The purpose of this chapter is to survey the different roads for the church being offered at the present time in both literature and practice. I've divided them into five broad categories or models, giving each a title borrowed or adapted from the commercial or industrial world. The choice of this kind of title is deliberate because, I believe, in different ways each of the approaches is influenced by recent trends in commerce or industry. Each of the models has something to offer but is not complete in itself. Each is first described and then critiqued as a way forward for the church at the present time in the hope of encouraging the reader to look for better ways.

The Church as a Chain of Cinemas

There is a view of the local congregation which sees the group of people who assemble for worship in a particular place on Sunday mornings as a random group of individuals who choose a service at that particular place and time for a variety of personal reasons much as people choose to go to a particular cinema (only a church attender would probably attend more regularly and on the same day of the week). The key attraction is what is offered 'from the front'. In order to increase the number of people who come, it's important to pay attention to the quality of the experience and, of course, to advertise the times of the services clearly.

On this view of a congregation, if the number of stipendiary clergy in a deanery or circuit is diminished, the approach to pastoral re-organisation is fairly straightforward (or so it seems at first). The most important priority is to staff the services on Sunday and, sometimes, during the week. This is done through a combination of increasing the expectations on the stipendiary clergy through staggering service times (8.00 a.m. at St Bertha's, 9.30 a.m. at St Agatha's four miles away, then back to St Bertha's for 11.00) and partly through seeking to train and deploy more volunteer and part-time ministers who can fulfil this role of leading Sunday worship.

As mentioned above (p. 25f.) a significant amount of thinking has been undertaken within the Church of England and in other denominations both about the changing role of stipendiary clergy and strategies for deployment. In the Anglican documents, the survey of diocesan strategies undertaken in 1998 found clear evidence of both vision and spirituality and 'a theological grounding of strategies using the theology of the Trinity, incarnation, mission and baptism' (although it is perhaps not insignificant that the theology of the church is missing from this list). 'Shaping Ministry for a Missionary Church' also finds as common themes (among others) that the Church of England is not retreating from its commitment to offer ministry to the whole community, a massive emphasis on teams and a trend towards larger structural units.[5] This creative new thinking is encouraging and is to be commended. However, many congregations still perceive that pastoral re-organisation is driven, in fact, as much by financial constraints as by a coherent theology of church and ministry. Often the situation is viewed through a particular set of spectacles:

- we need to keep the church going in its existing pattern of services
- therefore we need to reshape and reorder our resources for ministry to do this as well as possible.

Energy is therefore invested in turning as many lay people as possible into clergy or para-clergy whose main ministry is seen as maintaining this existing pattern of services. The advent of more col-laborative styles of ministry is sometimes seen as the source of the renewal of church life and of congregations. Collaborative ministry is a very good thing. But it is not enough on its own. If the problem is the way we are church then no amount of renewal of ministry only will solve it.[6]

There are at least three serious consequences to the move described above. The stipendiary clergy are becoming more and more stretched and face the additional demands of more hands-on work and the task of co-ordinating a large team of lay ministers. Both ordained and lay ministry becomes focused increasingly upon church-based activities, especially worship, and misses out on the vital aspect of service in the society and for the kingdom of God. Thirdly, as we shall see below, we are adopting structures of church life and ministry which may be good for the maintenance of congregations in decline but which are demonstrably very difficult as a basis for development and growth.

We need to begin with a much more radical question. What is the church called to be and to become and to be doing in our society at the present time? Only when we have some kind of answer to that question will we know how and why we should be shaping ministry.

Christian congregations must not be seen as random collections of individuals who gather together on Sunday mornings in a particular time and place. They are not. As we shall see in greater detail in Part Three, this is a massive distortion of what the church is called to be as that calling is expressed in Scripture and the Christian tradition. It is also a very misleading basis on which to see a local church with the complex, interlocked series of relationships which we call a community.

The most helpful way of describing churches as communities produced in recent years has been that of Arlin Rothauge, which has been adapted and built upon both by myself and others.[7] The majority of churches involved in the kind of changes in pastoral reorganisation described here will be small congregations operating as either family or pastoral churches (see Table 1).[8] For that reason a description of these two congregational types is reproduced on the following pages.

The largest number of churches in the United Kingdom fall into the first category of church, called by Rothauge the *Family Church*. A family church consists of a congregation of up to sixty people, although often the number involved will be less. In a family church, everyone in the congregation (more or less) knows everyone else. The feel of the church is that of an extended family. Often the key offices in the church are held by representatives of two or three human families or dynasties who pass on these roles among their own number. The family church is a durable structure, able to sustain itself through the ministries of different incumbents, who act (more or less) as chaplain to the family, being there at times of crisis to offer care and support but not entrusted with the leadership and direction of the group. However, despite their durability, family churches can be hard to join. This is partly because it takes a long time to feel that you belong: you need to know and to be known by the majority of the congregation. It is partly also because family churches need to guard their boundaries informally but carefully. Only those who meet with the approval of those who act as gatekeepers to the community will be welcomed to be permanent members.

Where a church grows and develops beyond this size and stage it is normally through making the transition to a *Pastoral Church* dynamic. For this to happen there needs to be an entrusting of some degree of power and responsibility to the minister by the key lay people in the congregation and a letting go by the congregation of the need to know everyone else. In the pastoral church, the key relationship is between each member of the congregation and the ordained minister. There is a high expectation on the minister of personal attention and care, particularly during times of crisis. The pastoral church is the easiest of all of these

The Family Church

- 1–50 members
- Dominated by a few human dynasties
- 'Gatekeepers'
- Minister as chaplain to the family

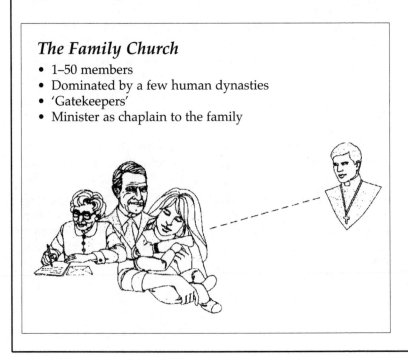

The Pastoral Church

- 50–150 members (100 adults)
- Minister is pastor to everyone
- High expectations of personal care
- Pastoral care ceiling

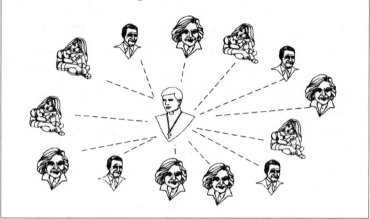

models of church to join: all that is needed to belong is a relationship with the pastor. My sense is that most small to medium-sized churches which are seeing growth in their congregations are growing into this kind of a church. However, pastoral churches are exceedingly vulnerable to changes in the minister. Each time there is a change a substantial proportion of the congregation will not make the transition to the new incumbent. Also, pastoral churches will continue to grow only until they reach their pastoral care ceiling. This is fixed at the incumbent's capacity to maintain relationships with every member of his or her congregation. Once that ceiling has been reached, new people may join the congregation but others will probably be leaving at an equal and balancing rate.

The level of this pastoral care ceiling will vary according to a number of variables but a hundred adults is a good guide figure. It may be a little lower or higher depending on the energy and vitality of the vicar; on the levels of need and deprivation in the area; and on the proportion of new Christians within the congregation. The addition of another ordained member of staff, such as a curate in a title post, will raise the ceiling typically by about thirty people. However the numbers attending church will probably fall again once that particular curate moves on. Once a church has reached its pastoral care ceiling, the minister in particular will tend to work at slightly more than capacity, particularly if he or she is also working and praying for the church to grow. It is at this point that clergy are most vulnerable to developing addictive patterns of behaviour in relation to their pastoral work. It is a heady thing indeed to be continually needed by a large congregation of different people and the temptation is to work long hours – and yet still find that all of the work cannot be done.

TABLE 1 Observations on Church Size[9]

40% of churches in England have congregations of 50 or less

64% have congregations of 100 or less

75% have congregations of 150 or less

The average size of an Anglican congregation in 1998 was 60

The average size of a Methodist congregation in 1998 was 61

However, 44% of Anglican and 41% of Free Church churchgoers attend just 11% of the churches giving some indication of the importance of the larger churches to the denominations as a whole.

There is a key difference between family churches and pastoral churches when it comes to resilience to change and potential growth and development. Family churches are very resilient to changes of ministers but are seldom able to change and grow. Pastoral churches are able to grow but are very susceptible to a change of ministers. Therefore:

- Where a full-time minister comes to a 'family church' there is the possibility and energy for significant growth and development. However, this rarely happens because of constraints on clergy deployment.
- Where two or more family churches are combined in pastoral re-organisation the result for the congregations is likely to be very little change in numbers initially but very little potential for growth. Given that all churches lose some members through people dying, becoming infirm or moving away from the area, the net result is likely to be a steady fall in membership. The strategy is therefore an appropriate one for maintenance or managing decline but inappropriate as a strategy for mission, growth and development.

- Where one or more pastoral churches are combined the result is very likely to be decline, sometimes quite rapid, to the dynamic of community which can be sustained by a congregation without a full-time minister – that of the family church as the following diagrams illustrate.

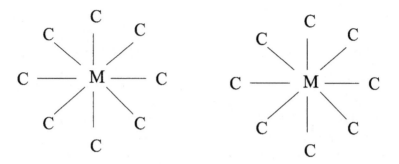

Figure 2.
Stage 1: Two pastoral churches each with their own minister.

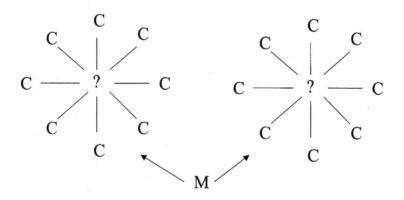

Figure 3.
Stage 2: The two churches combine sharing a minister in a chaplaincy role, largely for financial reasons. There is a vacuum at the centre of each of the churches where the minister used to be. The minister may attempt to compensate for this by over-working to meet unrealistic expectations of care and community.

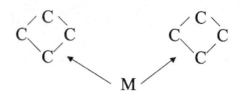

Figure 4.

Stage 3: If no attention is paid to the dynamics of community and pastoral care, the two congregations will decline to the point where they are self-sustaining, smaller, family-type congregations. The irony is that, in all probability, the amount of parish share paid by the diocese from the two congregations will also decline to half of the previous combined level and further pastoral re-organisation will then be necessary.[10]

In summary:

Scenario	Likely outcome
Full-time minister comes to family church	Growth
Two or more family churches combined	Steady decline
Two or more pastoral churches combined	Rapid decline

I am not arguing here that such decline is inevitable as part of pastoral re-organisation: only that it is highly likely if no attention is paid to the dynamics of community which operate within congregations and if churches are combined as if they are local outlets for a chain of cinemas.

As I have observed different forms of re-organisation taking place, there is very little awareness of these dynamics on the part of the congregations. The most normal (and understandable) response of a congregation to pastoral re-organisation is to expect things to continue more or less as they were before. The clergy struggle to make sense of what is happening to them and find themselves caught in a complex force-field of expectations. Those who have good skills of self-management and good networks of support are able to analyse what is happening and take steps to address the situation. Those who do not can be adversely affected by the increased workload and the inability to reconcile competing demands. Those responsible for the re-organisation often seem to have only a limited understanding of what is taking place and are therefore unable or unwilling to offer the training or support which is needed for transition. My principal point here is that we need to develop a much richer theological understanding of what the church is called to be as the basis for a strategy for ministry.

The Church as a Local Franchise

One of the most striking commercial developments of recent years has been the development of the franchise system of shops and restaurants. Instead of opening an independent local coffee shop and calling it 'Fred's Café', someone starting a business will enter into partnership with a major chain who will take care of design, image, product, market research, staff training and advertising. Everything is standardised from the menu to the salt packets and the napkins. The outlet opens as Starbucks or McDonald's and is, normally, instantly successful.

There is a way of seeing the local church which is influenced by the tremendous success of hamburger chains and coffee shops. In some ways it is an extension of the cinema model, since the main focus is likely to be on the quality of the experience of attending or belonging both on Sundays and during the week. The situation of church decline which has formed the backdrop to the Christian life in Great Britain over the last thirty years has led to something of a loss of confidence in what is local, what is offered by the established denominations, and, with some exceptions, to ideas which are generated within the UK. This in turn has led to a search for in-spiration and answers (or, more dangerously, *the* answer) from different contexts, of which the most dominant has been the Church in North America. In turn this has led to something of a 'franchise' approach to church life in which a local congregation gears their worship style, means of evangelism and nurture, philosophy of ministry, government and purpose towards a particular model which is **deemed** to be successful and effective. Some of the trends and external influences which have made their mark in this way have included the church growth movement, in the late 1980s,[11] the Seeker Services sponsored by the Willow Creek organisation,[12] the particular approach to worship, the gifts of the Spirit and church life promoted by the Vineyard through conferences and publications,[13] the Cell Church movement with its emphasis on mission-orientated small groups[14] (of which more below), and, most recently, the concept of the 'Purpose Driven Church' emanating from Saddleback Community Church in California and the Senior Pastor there, Rick Warren.[15]

All of these movements are from the evangelical wing of the Church (in slightly different places on the complex spectrum). This is partly, no doubt, something to do with my own perspective and awareness, yet it does seem to me that evangelicals are more open to these movements than are other sections of the Church. The pragmatic desire to discover and use something which works is stronger amongst evangelicals than other movements within Christianity.[16] However, there are other franchise-type movements, such as Cursillo[17] and RCIA,[18] which have influenced other parts of the established denominations in recent years. Some Anglican churches have begun to describe their life according to the particular 'brand' of nurture course they are using at the present time both in parish profiles for new appointments and even occasionally in advertisements or through belonging to a particular network or through members and ministers attending a particular conference.

I should say immediately that I think many of the movements mentioned have brought (and are bringing) good and significant things into the life of the Church in Great Britain, as have other movements and emphases which have emerged here. I have read the books, been to the conferences and, in some cases, bought the T-shirt. Many of the insights shared in this way have been gained at significant cost to the people themselves and are passed on with integrity and not for personal gain. We have many lessons to learn as a Church and need to be wide open to the perspectives of different traditions and of the world Church.

However, I am concerned at the degree to which some churches in the UK are keen to develop and to imitate others and adopt a franchise mentality, for the following reasons.

John Drane has argued in a recent book that this franchise mentality will lead to a serious stifling of creativity in the life of the Church.[19] Sociologists have described the phenomena associated with the franchise industry as 'McDonaldization'.[20] A key part of

McDonaldization is the emphasising of the four factors of efficiency, calculability, predictability and control. These four elements are essential for the effective transplanting and reduplication of a dining, shopping or church experience from one context to another. However, to emphasise these concepts in the life of the Church is also to reduce, suppress and squeeze out their opposites: freedom, variety, adaptability, creativity and spontaneity. Put these two sets of concepts side by side and ask the question whether the Holy Spirit has more to do with one column than the other. Drane's conclusion is that the Church must be aware of and resist the tendency towards franchising in our culture and I would acknowledge and endorse that insight.

Secondly, I have observed in the movements I have known best that the effective translation of something which works from one context to another is a complex process and involves a number of stages. First the originating church must discern accurately the reasons for the effectiveness of a particular strategy. Second, they must be able to describe and communicate that strategy clearly in a different context and situation. As a third stage in the process the receiving church must hear and understand what is being taught, locate it within an overall theological understanding and then have the skills to apply and translate what they have heard into practice. There is every possibility that what has originally been effective will be significantly distorted in this process of transmission and that what is both a theologically sound and effective strategy in one context may become a distorted over-emphasis which does not quite work in another.

A typical example of this distortion takes place when an emphasis or method for evangelism is separated from the accompanying statement of values about the life of the church. Many churches have 'borrowed' from Willow Creek the strategy and methods of seeker services as a tool in evangelism. Some have even borrowed this church's powerful mission statement: 'We want to turn irreligious people into fully devoted followers of Jesus Christ'. Yet, for many, this becomes separated from Willow Creek's primary vision and emphasis on becoming a Christian community with a particular quality of life expressed in the vision statement: 'We want to become a biblically functioning community'.[21] To engage in seeker sensitive evangelism without thinking through what it means to be church is unlikely to be effective or to develop a healthy community. Imitation is not an easy exercise for churches.

Thirdly, there is something about the nature of a local church which strongly suggests that we need to emphasise the particular as much as the general. All churches are called to be and to express the same values as part of their common life: to worship God; to proclaim the good news; to work for the kingdom of God in their own area and throughout the world. But this need not be in exactly the same way in each place. Different social contexts and cultures will mean that different approaches are necessary. Congregations are shaped by their history, spirituality, theological emphases, the dynamic of their community life and the gifts and people available to them. They may also discern a particular vocation or call from God which affects their life and mission. The vision and values which are borrowed from a different church tradition, culture and continent may be extremely helpful as a way of stimulating reflection and change within a British church context, as a worked example or a source for ideas, but they should not be transplanted uncritically and wholesale into a different context. Particular programmes, emphases, methods and materials might be adapted or adopted for similar tasks within the home context yet it is unlikely that any one model or situation will provide all that is needed.

At the beginning of the Book of Revelation, we find a collection of seven letters written in the name and person of Christ by the recipient of the vision to the 'angel' of each of seven key churches in what is now modern Turkey.[22] In the preface to the vision, the risen Christ is seen walking among the lampstands which represent the seven churches, watching over them. The churches are all of a similar age and were founded by the same apostles. They are all within a similar culture and would be in regular communication with one another. What is striking about the seven letters is their diversity. Most are commended but each for different virtues. Most are corrected, but each for different faults. This is individual analysis and prescription rather than a generic, franchise approach to church development – but analysis and prescription set within a common understanding of what the church is called to be.

The Church
as a Unit of Production

The three remaining models can be dealt with more briefly. A church is seen as a unit of production whenever its chief aim or vision is defined as quantifiable output and the life of the congregation is geared simply towards generating that output in a way which is efficient and sustainable. The most natural product or output for the church is, of course, seen to be the making of disciples. Any church which has a mission statement similar to the following is in danger of structuring its life in this way.

> This church exists to make disciples who make disciples

The Great Commission at the end of Matthew's Gospel is certainly something which every church needs to take seriously, as I shall argue below. However, to define and order the whole purpose and life of the church around this commission alone will lead to distortions in the Christian community which will not be life-giving to those who may be part of it. Nor, curiously, will this kind of church develop disciples of the type intended by Jesus in Matthew 28. It may be useful to draw an analogy with marriage. One of the highest purposes of Christian marriage is to provide a context for the birth and nurture of children.[23] Yet to make the birth and nurture of children the only purpose and mission of a Christian marriage is to distort the marriage relationship which has at its heart the mutual companionship, love, trust and growing unity of a man and a woman. Unless attention is paid to that growing relationship of husband and wife, the marriage is unlikely to provide an effective means for the nurture of children. In the same way, one of the highest callings of the church is to make disciples – yet if the making of disciples is made to be the chief and only purpose of the life of a community it will not be a healthy place in which to nurture new Christians.

Many of the movements referred to above as likely sources of the franchise within the evangelical community have been developed in a context of mission agencies or theological positions where the fulfilling of the Great Commission has been the paramount motivation shaping the life of the church. Although many of the authors have themselves moved on from that position to rediscover a much fuller understanding of what it means to be church, there is a resulting tension in the conferences, literature and application of the principles such that when they are translated into a new context, the fuller understanding of church is often left behind and the dominant concept of an evangelistically centred church remains. This is a particular danger with the cell church movement. The writings of its chief proponents, particularly Ralph Neighbour and William Beckham, contain a carefully developed, biblically based theology of what it means to be church. However, adaptations of the cell church material are prone to borrow the methods of evangelism and not base the life of the small groups on this richer theological foundation. Neighbour himself describes as the first two categories of reasons why cell churches run into difficulties in the following way:

1. The cells are not based upon a solid theological understanding of why they exist.
2. The pastors who develop cells are using them for the wrong motives. Cells developed to make a church grow will fail every time! Growth is never a goal – it's the natural by-product of doing something right! Where there's true community, there will be growth![24]

Quality Control

Neighbour's concept links neatly with the fourth way forward currently being explored. Over the past five years there has been a shift in direction in thinking being promoted by church growth specialists away from programmes which of themselves promote numerical growth and towards examining and developing the quality of community life within a particular congregation. The basic thesis is that churches grow by becoming better at what they do.

The chief proponent of this school of thinking is Christian Schwartz, who has developed a systematic way of testing churches against eight quality characteristics, defined as follows:[25]

- empowering leadership
- gift-orientated lay ministry
- passionate spirituality
- functional structures
- inspiring worship services
- holistic small groups
- need-orientated evangelism
- loving relationships.

Churches engaging in natural church development are encouraged to survey their members and to chart their score against each of these eight quality characteristics. This then gives those responsible a clear indication of where to begin to make improvements. Churches which achieve a score of 65 per cent or more in each category are likely to be growing numerically.

A related approach has also been developed through work undertaken in the Diocese of Durham by Dr Janet Hodgson, Adviser in Local Mission, and Robert Warren of Springboard.[26] Their work is based on observing the characteristics of healthy (rather than growing) churches and uses a slightly different list. A healthy church

1. has an energising faith
2. has an outward-looking focus
3. finds out what God wants it to do
4. faces the cost of change and growth
5. practises an enabling style of leadership
6. has a participative laity
7. is a loving community
8. sees discipleship as a lifelong journey of faith
9. practises what it preaches
10. does a few things well.

This is an excellent list of qualities. The Springboard approach is being widely used by churches as an audit tool to reflect upon the quality of their congregational life and to highlight particular areas for development, and has been taken on board by several dioceses.

Both Natural Church Development and the Hodgson/Warren work have produced useful tools for churches who want to reflect on the importance of their common life and assess its quality. Any kind of audit which yields accurate information about how a particular congregation is perceived by its own members has the potential to be helpful. A strength of both sets of material is the desire to see churches as organic and that the way things are in one part of a Christian community must affect the whole. I very much prefer the Hodgson/Warren approach of substituting the word 'healthy' for 'growing' and for not linking the congregational audit material with a programmatic way forward for each congregation (which tends to be the pattern adopted by Natural Church Development).

However, a potential weakness of both approaches seems to me to be the lack of a common and coherent understanding of what the church is and is called to be undergirding the audit. At one level, Natural Church Development at least could be read as promoting a list of qualities which make churches attractive to their members, pleasant and fulfilling to belong to, and which are therefore likely to grow in an increasingly mobile and consumer-driven society. This is a church in which I can have my needs met (including my need to participate in its leadership and find fulfilment through exercising my gifts in ministry). But is it a church which is likely to serve the needs of the poor; to take an unpopular stand on social issues; to invest significant amounts of time in areas of the community where there may be little immediate return? Where is the concern for the kingdom of God? Where is the concern for Christian unity and collaboration with other congregations? Where is the call to sacrifice and suffering for the sake of the gospel? Where is the failure which was as much a mark of the early Church as its success?

An approach to church life based largely or mainly on raising the quality of congregational life may be useful but will always be incomplete and should, of itself, carry something of a health warning. At its most basic, the quality control aspect of church life can be reduced to the slogan: a church which concentrates on meeting the needs of its members is most likely to grow. This is a long way from the gospel saying that those who want to save their life will lose it.[27]

The Church
as a Mirror of Society

A fifth and final model is that advocated by several recent authors who argue that since society is changing in certain ways, the church also must change in identical ways if it is to move out of decline and begin to thrive. Exponents of this approach in recent literature include Michael Moynagh, Eddie Gibbs and, to a lesser extent, Robin Greenwood in his most recent book.[28] Moynagh draws attention (among other things) to consumerism, choice and the tailor-made society, to the paradoxical development of different values for consumers and workers and the changing face of community, and draws lessons for the shape of the church in the future. Gibbs and Coffey analyse the changes brought by post-modernity and think creatively on the basis of this about the shape of church life and ministry. Greenwood examines theories of connectedness, gestalt and the global economy as key developments and finds ways of responding in the developing life of the church.[29]

Clearly the appeal of these authors to study, listen to and learn from contemporary culture needs to be heard. Yet we must also beware of a tendency in Moynagh and Gibbs to move too rapidly from this cultural listening to prescription for the church today without asking the more fundamental (and theological) questions about the nature and vocation of the church in every generation.

There will, no doubt, be some ways in which society is changing which are compatible with God's call to the church. But there will also be other ways in which society is changing which the church is called to resist: we are surely meant to be counter-cultural as well as moving with the flow. Such approaches may therefore be a source of ideas and helpful analysis of society, but they are unlikely to provide lasting solutions or a way forward.

Rehoboam faced a dilemma at Shechem right at the beginning of his reign. The choices he made would affect his own future and the future of his nation significantly. He received advice which was conflicting. In the same way we also stand at something of a cross-roads. The decisions we make will have serious consequences for the life of the church and for the life of our wider society. We cannot reconcile all the conflicting advice and pretend it is saying the same thing. A patient who is ill needs more than platitudes, hints and possibilities. I think it is unlikely that we can manage our way out of decline. The new emphasis on collaborative ministry in which the Church is making a huge investment is welcome but it does not address the core question of how we change the way that we are church. It is no use training new drivers if the engine of the bus has fallen out. It is unlikely that any single Christian community, course or franchise worldwide has the complete answer for the church in the UK. We need to bring the insights of Scripture and tradition to bear on the present situation as we seek a better way.

Can you think of examples of the way these models have influenced your own local church or others nearby?

What are the essential ingredients of a better way?

5

A Way
Forward?

Moses and the Tribes of Israel

The Book of Deuteronomy is cast as a series of speeches given by Moses to the tribes of Israel assembled beyond the Jordan as they prepare to enter the Promised Land. At the beginning of the book, Moses looks back and gives edited highlights of Israel's journey from slavery in Egypt to the threshold of conquest. The account is striking for what it does not mention: Deuteronomy makes no reference to the plagues or the exodus from Egypt, the crossing of the Red Sea, the tablets of the law, manna in the wilderness, the pillar of cloud or the pillar of fire. All of these incidents are assumed or alluded to but none is retold. Two incidents alone receive particular focus. The story of spying out the land is given at some length.[1] This is partly because it provides a context for the setting of the book but also because the story reinforces the message of the choice that lies before the people, which in turn is central to the theme of Deuteronomy. However, the first story to be retold in a simplified form is that of the appointment of the tribal leaders and the re-formation of the community.[2]

It is not immediately clear why this story in particular should stand at the head of the book except that the authors evidently considered it to contain a vital lesson for the people of God, not only for the generation of the Exodus and conquest but for their own day and in every age. It may also be a sign that Deuteronomy was compiled as a law book and reference point for the leaders and judges described here in every generation.

Here, and in the parallel and fuller account in Exodus, there is again a need for change in ordering the life of the people of God. As we saw in the story of Samuel, the present system is no longer working. In the account of the demand for a king in 1 Samuel 8, the need is for a greater centralisation of power and authority in a single person. Here the need which is identified through Jethro's visit is the opposite: for greater dispersal of power and authority and its vesting in a much broader range of people. In the account in Samuel, a combination of external changes is the driving force for new thinking ('Give us a king like other nations'). In Exodus/Deuteronomy the changing circumstances are internal. The people are emerging from conditions of slavery where they would have had only limited powers to settle disputes among themselves and to take collective decisions. They are therefore growing up into responsibility and government. Initially, great authority had been vested in Moses, who led them during a time of crisis as they escaped from captivity. However, the style of leadership that is appropriate for the exodus itself is no longer working during the time of wandering in the wilderness as the tribes make the transition to being an independent nation and a complete society. New structures are needed. Reference is made in both Exodus and Deuteronomy to the imbalance between the numbers of people and the resources available to guide them (whilst affirming that the increase itself is part of the blessing God has given):

> 'I am unable by myself to bear you. The Lord your God has multiplied you, so that today you are as numerous as the stars of heaven. May the Lord, the God of your ancestors, increase you a thousand times more and bless you, as he has promised you! But how can I bear the heavy burden of your disputes all by myself?'[3]

Unless some radical changes are made, the situation will become unbearable for both Moses and the people. Jethro's role is to help both Moses and the Israelites 'see' the problem (which they lived with each day but could not recognise).[4] An alternative vision is developed and placed before the people. This alternative is accepted and therefore: '... I took the leaders of your tribes, wise and reputable individuals, and installed them as leaders over you, commanders of thousands, commanders of hundreds, commanders of fifties, commanders of tens and officials, throughout all your tribes.'[5] Power and authority are devolved onto a much wider group of people, throughout the whole assembly. It is not enough simply to find a few assistants for Moses. A large number of people of recognised ability are chosen for the task. Basic guidelines are given to the judges and the law is taught to the whole people.[6] There is scope to refer difficult decisions to the next level and, in Exodus, to Moses himself. A much healthier ratio of leaders to people is established which is able to bring unity, purpose and quality of life to the tribes through their journey in the desert and through the period of conquest and settlement of the Promised Land.

The two passages from Exodus and Deuteronomy have clearly been influential within the later traditions of leadership development in the Bible. Nehemiah's plan for the rebuilding of the walls of Jerusalem owes something to this concept of the delegation of authority and tasks. Jesus himself models a ratio for care and disciple making of 1 to 12 which is similar to that of Moses and linked to the picture of the twelve tribes of Israel.[7] Luke's description of the choosing of the seven clearly owes something to the wisdom preserved in the Exodus and Deuteronomy narratives, as do other passages about the development of ministry in the early churches. As the Church through history and in modern times has reflected on the organisation of its common life, so this story has become important and influential in the tradition and in contemporary literature on re-ordering the life of the Christian community.[8]

Finding the Right Metaphor

As we have seen, the life of the church in Great Britain today is ready for change. Like other Christians before us, we may find part of the way forward in the story of Moses' re-organisation of the tribes. We too are wrestling with the question of the ratio between those called to guide and guard the people of God and the people themselves. We may be wrestling also with the challenges of seeing a community grow to maturity. The number of stipendiary clergy is falling in proportion to the Church as a whole, which itself is contributing to further decline. We too are addressing changes brought about by our wider context. We are less conscious than our parents and grandparents of being a stable and dominant Church within a nominally Christian society. We are correspondingly more conscious therefore of becoming a gathered community within that society. That gathered community can no longer borrow its internal structures from the society in which it lives but must develop its own.[9] We are therefore, in turn, more aware that we are on a journey together through unknown territory. Looking after a stable group of people in one place is one task. The pastoral situations requiring intervention or help are likely to be those concerned with personal change and development: adolescence, marriage, childbirth, illness, retirement and bereavement. Guiding a community on a journey requires structures of community and ministry which are able to fulfil this first role yet also deal with a new set of issues concerned with the common life. These include such issues as gathering and enabling community, nurturing a common identity and vocation, discerning a way forward, judging the pace of change, helping the community adjust to growth or decline, creating space for newcomers, and so on.

The purpose of this chapter is to attempt to summarise and describe a way forward for the church at the present time which the remainder of the book will flesh out, test and explore. As will be apparent, my own description of this way forward builds on, describes and develops a number of common threads in the work of those who have attempted the task before me. These roots and foundations are explored in the following chapter. We are seeking a way of being church in the local context which is both sustainable and holds the possibility of growth and development. We are seeking a way of being church which is rooted in our actual circumstances but which is informed, shaped, refreshed and renewed by Scripture and the Christian tradition. Before we attempt that task, it is important to be clear about two preliminary points.

The general and the particular

The first is the relationship between the general and the particular. As we have seen, one approach to our present situation has been to attempt to define very rigidly the route to becoming a fruitful or successful church, in a similar model to the franchise industry. As much as possible about the way to do church is thought through in advance, defined, described, packaged and put into practice in the local situation. As we have seen, this approach is the opposite of true subsidiarity and tends to stifle the creative work of the Spirit and of individuals and communities. It also takes away the concept of differences between contexts and particular vocations upon groups of Christians. I would argue therefore that the franchise model is not the way for a church to develop to maturity or, therefore, in the number of disciples. In standardising and packaging the format for God's people we are in danger of taking away something of what it means to *be* God's people.

The opposite of the franchise route, which stifles the particular at the expense of the general, is to attempt to say that there may be no recognisably uniform way forward. Robert Warren has argued in his influential book *Building Missionary Congregations*:

> Here our starting point must be to establish the fact that there are many alternatives. Such a notion is in conflict with the conventional wisdom that our present way of operating, namely the normal parish church, is the only way of being church ... In a period of transition, we would be wise to 'let a thousand flowers bloom'.[10]

If the franchise model has the weakness of giving people too much, the opposite approach has the balancing weakness of providing too little. If every congregation and parish is to develop in its own way, then each must certainly go through the demanding process of learning and reflection on what it means to be church. However, the evidence suggests that some guidance is also needed in many contexts for a congregation to find a workable and sustainable way forward. Moreover, if there is no commonly owned or articulated vision of what a framework for the local church might be, this process is likely to need to be repeated at every change of minister, every time there is pastoral re-organisation and every time the diocese or denomination produces a new strategy. This would be wasteful and may not be effective in the long term. In the period since *Building Missionary Congregations* was written, there has been only a limited blossoming of different models of being church but that is still set against the general background of malaise and decline. I want to argue here for a middle way: a framework for understanding how the life of any local church might develop in the present context which gives a vision of how things might move forward without being over specific.

The trellis is not the vine

In all discussions of this kind, great care must be taken to distinguish between the life of the church and the framework which supports and enables that life and growth. The life of a Christian community is both organic, part of its very being, and a grace conferred by the Spirit. The structures of ministry and community in a local church do not of themselves confer and give this gift of life, no matter how well thought out they may be. The bare bones assembled in the valley in Ezekiel's vision had no life in them until the Spirit was given to them. But that does not mean that the bones are unimportant to the body. To change the picture, to get the most from a vine or a young fruit tree, the branches need to be carefully cultivated and supported by wires or by a trellis. The trellis is not a living thing. It is not the vine. Yet it lends structure, support and order around which the living plant can grow and become fruitful.

The 'trellis' which the Church of England and many other churches have employed as the basic framework for church life is that of the single parish church and the stipendiary minister. Whilst this trellis is still effective in some situations, in very many contexts an important part of that trellis has now been eroded or taken away. Because of wider cultural factors, it may no longer be the most appropriate framework in any case even if it was sustainable. New structures are required. In general terms, denominations and dioceses have responded to this situation by seeking to provide only a framework for managing limited resources for ordained ministry within a wider geographical context such as the circuit or deanery. What is required is for a new kind of trellis to be extended to the local level in such a way as to enable and give new shape and support to the life of small communities within the congregations.

Transforming Communities

One of the keys to developing, ordering and enabling the life of the people of God through the local church is therefore to seek to put in place the right kind of trellis to enable both community and ministry to be well ordered. This will mean providing an adaptable, flexible framework that enables the life of the Spirit to be manifest in different ways in different contexts. This framework must:

- be appropriate theologically, given the nature of the Christian church.
- be sustainable given the resources for ministry available.
- have the capacity to give stability to vulnerable communities.
- resource the mission of the whole Church to our wider society, including the call to make disciples. There must, therefore, be the potential for growth.

For a common framework to grow up alongside and within existing parish or circuit structures, it must transfer easily to different social contexts (including very urban and very rural) and to different sizes of church (from the very large to the very small). It must also be owned by both the local church and the wider denomination in order to give continuity to the churches' life and mission during periods of pastoral re-organisation and changes of stipendiary minister.

The central argument of this book is that the basic building block of the local church, alongside the congregation, should be the small group of Christian people who together form a transforming community. The purpose of the community when it meets is to worship God, to build relationships with one another as the Body of Christ, to learn together and to support the ministry of each member of the community in the whole of their lives. Sometimes, this outward dimension of the group's life may also be expressed through undertaking a common task. An example of what a transforming community might look like in practice is given in the story at the beginning of the book. The concept of a transforming community is offered as a way of catching and articulating that dimension of the church's life which is caught by Jesus' travels with the disciples, by the early Christian house churches, by the monastic communities, by Methodist class meetings, by the house group movement of the

71

twentieth century, and by the cell church and base ecclesial community movements of the world Church. It is my contention that the malaise of the church in the mainstream denominations is due at least in part to a neglect of that aspect of church life which can be expressed in these small communities: depth of friendship and relationship; discipleship within structures of mutual accountability; worship and prayer which arise from and are closely related to shared lives; and a common sense of purpose enabling one another to share in the mission of God. I would argue further that the renewal of the church will come not through the re-organisation of ministry to serve existing structures but through the renewal of the whole Church in relationship and community.

The concept of the transforming community offers a flexible way forward which can be interpreted differently in each local situation. At the heart of what it means to be church is a call to enter into relationship with God and relationship with others which is meaningful, purposeful and mutually supportive and in which energy can be directed to a common end. Yet many people find it hard to discover such relationships in existing, established congregations. Something more is needed.

Styles of Community

If a local church is to discern its vocation and to develop its life with freedom, spontaneity and creativity, it will be important not to be over-prescriptive about how to develop this small group dimension of church life. The test is not the way things appear on the surface but the quality of relationships, prayer, learning and mission which is enabled through existing or developing networks of community. Three basic styles of transforming communities might be envisaged:

Intentional communities like those described in the story at the beginning of the book. These are groups nurtured into life deliberately because the church in a particular context is seeking the renewal of community and mission through small groups. They are formed with the particular intention of deepening relationships, worship and mission through their common life. Intentional communities will have a membership of between six and fifteen people. The ideal number is eight to ten (as we will explore below). They will agree together to meet regularly at a given interval (from every week to every month). An intentional community will have designated leaders who will attempt to guide and guard the life of the group. These leaders in turn may be part of a support and training network within the congregation or group of congregations. An intentional community will aim, as part of its common life, to worship and pray together; to enable Christian fellowship and mutual support; to learn and grow together in Christian discipleship and to express its life in terms of mission: both through enabling each member to live out their Christian faith in the whole of their life and through undertaking short-term mission projects together. It will have some kind of life-cycle or development cycle. Such communities do not come into being overnight. They are formed through the careful investment of time and energy by leaders and members and, usually, need to learn through experience how to grow together in this way. Intentional communities may grow into very stable groups of Christian people who meet together for many years. They may grow and therefore need to multiply and begin again. They may, through different circumstances, come to an end with their members joining other groups.

In many congregations, most of the intentional transforming communities will be made up of a cross section of adult members of the church. However, there may be some groups which meet during the daytime, and are therefore made up mainly of the retired or those at home with young children. There are some communities, led by adults, which are for children and young people with the same purposes of worship, building community and enabling ministry to the whole of life. In some contexts, there may be groups with a special focus in terms of their common mission: a group made up of teachers, health care workers or single parents. Most groups will meet together regularly as the most natural way of maintaining relationships. Others meet less frequently because of the different demands upon their time. Within the same church, each group will develop its own style and pattern of meeting together. Material for study is provided from time to time by the parish and links with Sunday worship through its themes.

Existing formal and informal communities already exist in many places disguised as branches of the Mothers' Union, or Parish Fellowships, Church Walking groups, choirs and bell ringers. What these groups already provide in terms of stable networks of relationships and ways of belonging is very valuable. Some may be open to the careful extending and deepening of some aspects of their common life so as to reflect more of what the contemporary church needs from its small communities. Others might be quite resistant to this. Yet there is little to be gained from intentionally closing such organisations when they might be life-bringing and sustaining for those within them and they have the capacity to produce the kind of community which is needed.

Associational networks form a third way of relationship and belonging. Community exists in many different guises, not all of which look like a formal house group. Sometimes a congregation or group within a congregation will have come to know one another extremely well through the years through sharing in an annual cycle of events which build community as a kind of bi-product (such as working together on a dramatic production or an annual bazaar or through organising and sharing in a parish holiday). Others will know one another well because they meet together regularly at lunch clubs for the elderly or meet each day at the school gate. In the past, groups of men and women from a congregation might have shared a shift in the mills, mines or factories. Here there are no structures for maintaining community which can be observed or duplicated but real community nevertheless exists. Again, these relationships need to be treasured and affirmed. However, it also needs to be recognised that in most contexts the circumstances which gave rise to this community occur now only rarely. Residential neighbourhoods are becoming less a focus of relationships; groups of people in the same area no longer work for the same employer; the regular rhythms of parish life of twenty years ago are disrupted by the mobility of modern society. Communities which have been built in these ways may satisfy those who are part of them now but tend to be inaccessible to those coming into the church whether as new Christians or existing Christians moving into the area. Churches which depend only on these associational networks for the formation of community are therefore restricting their membership to their present (usually ageing) congregations.

Guiding
Transforming Communities

The life of a transforming community is guided and guarded by a lay minister (or ministers) who see it as part of his or her vocation to enable the life of the group. The role of this minister is not to teach and to care for the group members but to facilitate the life of the group so that there is development in worship and prayer, in discipleship, in mutual care and relationship, in the mission of each member and of the community as a whole. The calling and gifts of this minister have been recognised by the wider congregation. The church centrally, through its ordained and lay ministers, provides the enablers of the transforming communities with guidance and support specific to the developing needs of the group as well as with more general training and opportunity for reflection with others fulfilling the same role and vocational support. Different members of the groups facilitate and lead different parts of the group meetings and the overall life of the community.

Nurture and Growth

There is the capacity for growth and renewal as disciples are made and new communities formed through:

- the growth of existing groups as new people are welcomed in, perhaps newcomers to the church or area or those who have come to faith or are growing in faith. The small group gives birth to a new community.
- the establishing of new communities as evangelism and nurture takes place through programmes offered by a church or group of churches. Groups formed for enquirers and new Christians grow together into new transforming communities.
- the planting of new transforming communities through two or more people attempting to grow a new group in a particular geographical area or among a network of people in a workplace or social group.

Congregations
and Small Communities

The extent to which different features in the life of the church are devolved onto smaller communities has varied. Sometimes these smaller groups have had a single explicit function expressed in the name of the group such as prayer groups or fellowship groups (although, undoubtedly a prayer group is always about more than simply praying together). At the other extreme, in some ways of being church, the small group becomes the primary or even the only expression of corporate church life: all the necessary dynamics of church are concentrated into its life together.

Growing the life of the congregation around the trellis of transforming community is midway between the two. The different aspects of church life are mostly not distributed between the public congregation and the small group meeting but rather manifested in different ways in each of them.

Worship takes place in one way in the larger congregation and another way in the small group. In the congregation, worship is in a public place, advertised to all and (hopefully) open and accessible to all. The congregation is the place where the Word of God is publicly proclaimed and where the sacraments of Holy Communion and baptism are celebrated. There seems no doubt that from earliest times Christians met and worshipped in public places and this is a vital feature of their common life.[11] However, they clearly also met in smaller communities in private homes not simply because of the constraints of persecution but because of different values which could be embraced and expressed in worship, particularly the way in which worship arises from the concerns of shared lives. In a small group, worship can be informed more directly by the experiences of group members; there can be prayer for individual needs; listening to the Word of God is about sharing reflections upon a text; there is the opportunity for every person to make some contribution to what is offered.

Christian fellowship, similarly, takes one form within the small group, another within a larger congregation. When a church meets publicly, fellowship is necessarily open and hospitable. All are welcome, from every section of society. In most cultures, as larger numbers gather together, there is a necessary formality but also the possibility of forming relationships across a wide spectrum of ages and social backgrounds. Children and elderly people, singles and families, men and women, different races and cultures might all be represented. A larger assembly is necessary to represent the whole richness of human society. However, larger assemblies are not good at fostering depth and intimacy within human relationships. Trust and confidentiality are essential parts of Christian fellowship that enable mutual support and community, and these cannot be achieved in a group which is wide open to anyone. Some expressions of small community serve to support people in particular need to enable them in particular forms of mission. In this way, a transforming community might consist largely of retired people (from inclination or convenience); of those who work in a particular place (because of the location); of just men or just women (for better mutual support and fellowship); of those engaged in a particular profession or ministry such as doctors or youth workers (for better support). Both dimensions are needed in order to express what it means to be church. A small community alone is not enough. How can we be the Christian church without children or the elderly? Yet a congregation alone is not sufficient either. How can we be the Christian church when our conversation remains at the polite and superficial level Sunday by Sunday?

Christian learning and discipleship is likely to take one form in the context of public worship as we learn through preaching prepared by those who have invested time in training and preparation, through songs led by highly trained musicians and carefully crafted hymns and liturgies. In this larger context we are able to be anonymous learners. We do not need to engage, nor is there any degree of accountability. In the context of a small community, however, Christian learning is about coming together to Scripture and sharing our reflections, with the guidance of the Holy Spirit; about offering what we ourselves can bring by way of insight, encouragement, testimony; about using natural, spontaneous human expression and conversational prayer. Others know us well enough to be aware whether there is a major conflict between what we profess and the people we are.

Finally, *Christian mission* also is expressed differently in each context. The different expressions are complementary and each needs the other. At the heart of Christian mission is the enabling of disciples to live out their faith in the context of the whole of their lives and encouraging them to discover their own gifts, vocation and way of expressing and sharing in God's love for the world. This enabling can be encouraged in a general sense when a congregation meets as a large group (and there is always a responsibility in preaching to keep a congregation's horizon very wide). However, this kind of mutual encouragement is most effective when it takes place in a small group and there is a degree of accountability both in respect of discipleship and living out our faith. As described in my opening story, devolving the responsibility of mission onto small communities would mean, in most churches, that much more, and more varied, missionary activity would take place in a given year, although much may well be hidden from view. Small communities certainly need the mission dimension to their life if they are to fulfil their potential. We form one kind of relationship when we are sitting in a circle facing one another and a different kind when we are working side by side on a common task. However, this does not mean that a congregation does not have a necessary missionary task also. There are some things which are better done by individuals or small groups. Others can be better facilitated by a local church acting as an institution within a local community. Its lay and ordained representatives may be duly appointed to (for example) the governing bodies of schools, hospitals or prisons. Alternatively, the church may be involved in redevelopment agencies or work in partnership with social services and other statutory or voluntary bodies in the relief of distress and poverty and the building up of our wider society. In a similar way, any local expression of the church in a congregation needs to relate to the wider Church both through its own denominational structures and ecumenically. For every small group to take on this responsibility would be unworkable.

This distribution of what it means to be church between the congregation and the small community is summarised in the following table.

Table 2

	CONGREGATION	**SMALL COMMUNITY**
WORSHIP	Public place, open to all	Home, by invitation (but all are welcome)
	Public proclamation	Reflection on particular context
	Celebration of the sacraments of Baptism and Eucharist	Prayer for individual members
		Worship arising from shared lives
FELLOWSHIP	Open, hospitable to all	Trust and confidentiality
	A wide cross section of society	Deeper relationships and mutual support
		Similar or more restricted groups
LEARNING	Trained preachers who have given time to preparation	The insights of a whole group coming to Scripture
	Carefully prepared words in songs and prayers	Unprepared wisdom, insight and testimony
	High standards in music and presentation	Using and valuing each person's gift
MISSION	Extending the horizon	Enabling mission by every member in the whole of life:
	Church acting as institution in society	work
	Partnerships with other agencies	family
		wider society
	Large, long-term projects	Small, short-term projects
	Relating to denomination and ecumenically	

Transforming Communities and Contemporary Culture

This framework of small communities I am proposing fits with different patterns of relating which already exist in contemporary culture. People clearly need to belong in different ways. Some need to be able to come and go, to be only loosely committed, to express their faith and interest on their own terms. A church which offers public worship services enables this possibility of informal belonging. However, for it to be available to our wider society, there needs to be a genuine community at the heart of the congregation. A church which only enables and encourages its members to belong in this way will rapidly become a very diffuse organisation with little sense of a centre. In previous generations that sense of belonging might have been facilitated by a full-time minister. It now needs to be generated by the intentional formation of community.

However, others in our society are seeking a different and more demanding way of belonging. They are looking for community, relationship and closer contact with people which can be in very short supply in our highly mobile society in which both work and leisure have become privatised and individualised. A church which offers these smaller communities provides this deeper, more committed way of belonging. For an individual, either way should be possible without the other, at least as a beginning to a life of Christian faith.

However, developing the life of a church by enabling small communities is also very counter-cultural. In a society which is consumer driven and likes to belong on its own terms, this way of being church emphasises a deeper call to discipleship, accountability, mutual responsibility for the life and health of a small group and shared responsibility for aspects of Christian mission. Its message will not always be popular. Keeping the larger dimension will, similarly, be counter-cultural to those who too easily become drawn into a small group which becomes introverted and quickly sees itself as near the heart of the purposes of God, if not the centre of the spiritual drama of the universe.

Transforming Communities in Different Contexts

The final section of this chapter attempts to explore how this concept of transforming communities might enable the life of the church in a number of different contexts. The following symbol is used for a transforming community in the illustrations which follow:

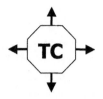

Each scenario also envisages that the life of the church or churches is guided and guarded not by an individual stipendiary minister but by a collaborative ministry team, expressing a diversity of gifts and sharing a common life.[12]

A network of small congregations

A small congregation in an urban or rural area structures its life as a single transforming community. Services on Sunday and/or mid-week events are shaped so as to provide opportunity to worship, to build relationships with one another and to support the ministry of each member through the whole of their lives. A major part of the task of the ordained minister is to nurture this transforming community within the six or seven small congregations committed to his or her care (Figure 5).

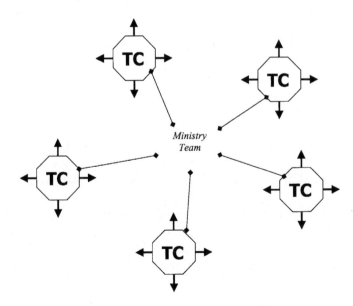

Figure 5.

Medium-sized congregation

A medium-sized congregation (60–120), when it meets together Sunday by Sunday, is made up of several of these smaller transforming communities. Not everyone who attends church is formally part of such a group: there are some who don't wish to belong in this way. However, it is the three or four transforming communities which nurture the relationships and shared discipleship of the church as a whole. Figure 2 shows that this medium-sized congregation has now been combined with a small neighbouring parish. Instead of attempting to guide both churches in the old model, the ministry team seek to nurture a single transforming community at the heart of the new parish, alongside their existing structures of community in the medium-sized congregation.

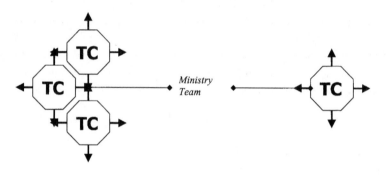

Figure 6.

'Minster' church

Figure 7 shows the different model of a group of churches where one has been designated as a 'minster' church for the area. Resources are concentrated here in order to reach out more effectively to the wider society and sustain the smaller congregations in their own mission. In the minster church itself, nurture courses are offered centrally and become, in time, a way of founding new transforming communities. In the smaller congregations, opportunities for the nurture of new Christians are taken through the existing transforming communities.

Figure 7.

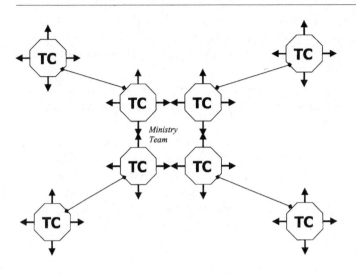

Larger congregation

Finally, a larger congregation (120+) is likely to be made up of even more of these smaller transforming communities, possibly with a much more intentional network of community and support for the ministers who guide their life (Figure 8).

Figure 8.

This larger congregation offers a nurture group centrally once or

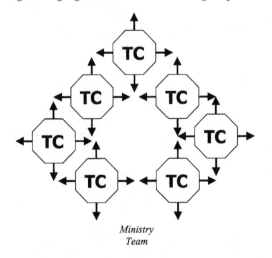

*Ministry
Team*

twice a year for those who are enquirers or new to the faith.

Normally, this nurture group itself becomes a transforming community after the first six months of its life. As the congregation grows in size, the structures of community and mission grow to keep pace.

In each of these contexts, the framework of transforming communities is able to provide stability during changes in the ordained ministry which come either through changes of personnel or pastoral re-organisation, providing that the church or group of churches continues to work to a common model of ordering its life. Each member of a small group is being supported and resourced in the whole of their life and ministry, therefore these communities have the potential to transform not only for the individuals who are part of them but for thousands of homes, schools, workplaces, hospitals, and voluntary contexts.

Describe to one another your impression of transforming communities from this chapter.

Does it seem like an appropriate way forward?

6

Foundations, Roots and Resources

Jesus went up on a mountainside and called to him those he wanted, and they came to him. He appointed twelve – designating them apostles – that they might be with him and that he might send them out to preach.[1]

Theological Foundations

As we saw in Chapter Three, the renewal of hope and vision for Christian people comes not simply from looking at our present situation (which may be very difficult) but from examining our present context in the light of the whole of the Christian tradition. New hope comes not from simply examining the problems we face but by looking at them in the light of eternity. As we look closely at reality on the one hand and at the calling of the church in the light of Scripture on the other, new vision and new possibilities emerge. In the process of this continual reformation in the life of the church, Christians move on not through original and new ideas, but through rediscovering and refreshing our understanding of different aspects of our tradition which have become lost or neglected in a particular context. In this way, the ecumenical movement was born out of a rediscovery of the call of Jesus for his Church to be one; the Charismatic movement out of a renewed desire for personal experience of the power of God. Both of these elements have always been part of the Christian faith and the Christian tradition but, over time, had become forgotten or neglected and needed to be restored to their rightful place. In the same way, seeking the renewal of the structures of church life through small communities should not be seen as some revolutionary new development but as the restoration of an aspect of the Christian faith which has always been present in the tradition, which has to some degree become neglected through historical circumstances and which now needs to be restored intentionally to the life of the Christian community if the church is to be effective in contemporary society. This chapter explores the presence of these ideas of Christian community within Scripture and the Christian tradition and begins by making explicit three important theological foundations to this developing understanding of what it means to be church.

The ministry of all the baptised

Jesus calls all those who follow him to a life of self-denial and of service.[2] Christian discipleship is to be lived out in the whole of one's life. In Romans 12, Paul uses the vivid image of a sacrifice being laid on the altar to describe the continual laying down of a Christian life in the service of God: 'I appeal to you therefore, brothers and sisters, by the mercies of God, to present your bodies as a living sacrifice, holy and acceptable to God, which is your spiritual worship.'[3] This calling to be a living sacrifice is worked out in different ways in different people, according to the differing gifts given to each. But there is no doubt in the biblical witness that the call to Christian discipleship is a call to the offering of the whole of our lives in response to the grace and gift of God in and through Jesus Christ. The New Testament does not envisage two classes of Christians: one active and one passive, one fully committed and one rather half-hearted. Although every church is called to be open, welcoming and accessible to strangers, to the uncommitted and to those whose faith is wavering, the basic building blocks and structures of our corporate life must be such as to enable those who are fully committed in their discipleship to grow and develop.

Baptism is, for the Christian, the sign of this radical new beginning and complete offering of oneself to God. The act of baptism by complete immersion contains the double symbolism of complete cleansing and of dying and rising again:

> Do you not know that all of us who have been baptized into Christ Jesus were baptized into his death? Therefore we have

been buried with him by baptism into death, so that, just as Christ was raised from the dead by the glory of the Father, so we too might walk in newness of life.[4]

Baptism is the foundation for and leads into the offering of one's life in service:

Those baptised are called upon to reflect the glory of the Lord as they are transformed by the power of the Holy Spirit, into his likeness, with ever increasing splendour (II Cor. 3:18). The life of the Christian is necessarily one of continuing struggle, yet also of continuing experience of grace. In this new relationship, the baptized live for the sake of Christ, of his Church and of the world which he loves, while they wait in hope for the manifestation of God's new creation and for the time when God will be all in all (Rom. 8.18-24; I Cor. 15.22-28, 49-57).[5]

This emphasis on baptism as the offering of the whole of our lives is reflected in recent revisions of the baptism service, particularly in the words of commission and promises made by the newly baptised:

Will you commit yourself to the Christian life of worship and service and be open to the renewing power of God?
Answer: With the help of God I will.
Will you seek the strength of God's Spirit as you accept the cost of following Jesus Christ in your daily life?
Answer: With the help of God I will.
Will you witness, by word and deed, to the good news of God in Christ, and so bring glory to God?
Answer: With the help of God I will.[6]

The Covenant Service of the Methodist Church catches superbly this sense of every disciple offering themselves to God in the whole of their lives. In the words of the covenant prayer:

I am no longer my own but yours.
Put me to what you will,
rank me with whom you will;
put me to doing, put me to suffering;
let me be employed for you or laid aside for you,
exalted for you or brought low for you;
let me be full, let me be empty,

> let me have all things, let me have nothing;
> I freely and wholeheartedly yield all things
> to your pleasure and disposal.[7]

Both Roman Catholic and the Protestant Churches have made enormous strides since the middle of the last century in recovering and developing this concept of the ministry of the whole people of God linked with the recovery of a richer understanding of baptism.[8] The development has vital implications for the ordering of the life of the church. All are called to offer the whole of their lives to God. Ministry is to be exercised by all, not simply by some. The structures of the life of the local church, therefore, must be such that they have the potential to build, exercise, maintain and develop the Christian service of the whole community, not simply the ministry of those called to be clergy or licensed ministers within the congregation. The local church must also, therefore, pay a very great deal of attention to models and patterns of Christian nurture such that all disciples are able to take up the responsibilities of ministry to which they are called through baptism.

Only a way of being church that takes seriously the transforming nature of small communities is able to provide a structure for on-going nurture and discipleship, for the recognition of gifts, vocation and ministry, and the context to support Christians as they offer their lives in Christian service.

Throughout Christian history there has undoubtedly been a tension between the imperative of Christian service and hospitality on the one hand, which seeks to serve all people where they are and at their point of need, and presenting the demands of Christian discipleship on the other hand, summed up in Christ's call to be prepared to leave everything for the sake of the gospel. From the time of Jesus and the apostles, the church has found it difficult if not impossible to express both of these dimensions of its common life in a single context. In his public teaching and in the feeding of the multitudes Jesus demonstrates service, hospitality and welcome with an invitation to all to follow and to go further. In his private encounter with the disciples, Jesus explores in more depth what Christian discipleship is to mean. In contemporary society, the church too needs to provide a context in which people can come and worship on their own terms, in their own way, a place to explore

Christian faith, to visit and to look in from the outside, without commitment. That context is offered through the provision of public worship and through other events. Yet we also need to provide a context for growth in discipleship, for encounter, for accountability, where commitment can be encouraged, nurtured and sustained and where ministry can grow. Many of our churches at present have the first but not the second. The balance needs to be restored.

The horizon of ministry is the kingdom of God

This ministry of the whole people of God is not to be exercised within and on behalf of the Church only. God loves the world, the whole world, not just the Church. The mission of God, in which the Church is called to share, is an expression of God's love and is a mission to the whole of creation and the whole of human society.

The Gospels describe Jesus proclaiming the kingdom of God or the reign of God.[9] Anyone writing or thinking about the church must continually bear in mind that the Greek word for 'church', *ekklesia*, is found only twice in the whole of the Gospel[10] whilst the phrase 'kingdom of God' or 'kingdom of heaven' occurs on scores of occasions.[11]

The phrase itself is a kind of shorthand coined by Jesus to sum up the way God intends things to be in human society and the way they will be one day. There is a great deal of teaching in the Old Testament about the kingship or reign of God and the conditions that prevail where God reigns. Much of the vision of the future in the prophets concerns the time when God's order and rule will prevail. At its best, and as Jesus uses the term, the vision is as wide as creation and extends through the whole of time. God's concern is not for one group of people within society, whether the Israelites, the Jews or the Christians, but for the ordering of the life of the whole world. Hence a concern for the kingdom of God means a concern for justice to prevail; a concern for the poor; a concern for the structures of society; a concern for ethical business practice and investment; a concern for the care of the elderly, the sick and the mentally ill; for prisoners, refugees and asylum seekers; for those forgotten by our wider society; and for the environment.

The five marks of mission adopted by the Bishops of the Anglican Communion express this kingdom horizon as they describe the call of the Church in participating in the mission of God as:

To proclaim the Good News of the Kingdom
To teach, nurture and baptise new believers
To respond to human need by loving service
To seek to transform unjust structures of society
To strive to safeguard the integrity of creation and sustain and
renew the earth.[12]

Our understanding of the ministry of all the baptised must be set
against this wider horizon of the kingdom of God. Ministry is meant
to be lived out and applied in the whole of human life. However,
much of the debate in recent years about ministry has been understandably pulled towards expressing Christian service primarily
within the life of the congregation. Emerging structures tend to focus
either on ways of sustaining the congregation as it is or upon the
part of mission which is making disciples rather than enabling the
ministry of all the baptised to the whole of society and the whole of
our lives. We need to resist this tendency and attempt to develop
ways of being church which release energy for ministry beyond the
congregation for the sake of the kingdom of God.

The model of church explored here attempts to keep the focus on
mission and ministry upon the whole of life, not simply the life of
the church. Most of us need help in order to think through the
implications of our Christian faith for the different contexts in which
we live and work. The church as it is presently structured does not
have a very good record in helping us to do that. Meeting together
in smaller transforming communities offers the possibility that more
can happen in this area through informal mutual encouragement;
through prayer for one another; through telling stories to each other
about how faith makes a difference or creates dilemmas; through
taking action together so that the whole community is involved in
some projects for the sake of the kingdom.

In order for this to happen, two things are vital. Mission needs to
be placed at the heart of the life of the small communities and kept
there. Models of small group life in the recent past have tended to
leave 'mission' to the wider congregation and have therefore become
somewhat stagnant and inward looking. Secondly, the model of mission that is placed at the heart of these small communities must be
as broad and long and high and deep as the love of God and not
restricted simply to one aspect (such as the making of disciples or

the sustaining of church life). Only then can the groups focus on enabling all its members to fulfil their own discipleship in every part of their life: at home, at work, through community ventures and in other ways. Only then can each group be set free to explore its own vocation in terms of short-term mission projects. This aspect of the communities' life must be given time and space when the group meets together through formal and informal conversations; learning and discipleship; time given over to practical planning and, in the case of mission projects, time, energy and resources applied to common tasks. In all of this the sensitive guiding of the groups themselves and of those who lead them will be a vital task.

The rhythm of worship and mission

When Jesus is asked to name the greatest commandment, he will not be tied to a single answer but gives a twofold reply:

> 'The first is, "Hear, O Israel: the Lord our God, the Lord is one; you shall love the Lord your God with all your heart, and with all your soul, and with all your mind, and with all your strength." The second is this, "You shall love your neighbour as yourself." There is no other commandment greater than these.'[13]

There is a balance and a rhythm in the Christian life between loving God expressed in our worship, which refreshes, renews and sustains our identity, and loving our neighbour, expressed in mission according to our particular gifts. When Jesus gathers the group of twelve disciples, he calls them 'to be with him, and to be sent out to proclaim the message'.[14] The pattern of the life in the Gospels, as far as the disciples are concerned, is expressed in this rhythm of being with Jesus and being sent out by Jesus. The picture is not one of spending years only in the company of other disciples and then years of continuous service and mission. Rather it is a rhythm of going out in service and proclamation and coming back together for periods of re-orientation, refreshment and reflection.

The same picture emerges from Acts and the Epistles. The apostles do not travel alone but in small groups, able to sustain one another along the way. They do not simply seek the conversion of individual Christians, saving souls for heaven. Instead, they intentionally form the new converts into Christian communities that are able both to build up and sustain the new disciples and become in turn centres for ongoing mission and ministry. The great sacrament of the Eucharist has this rhythm at the heart of its life. The Christian community comes together to be built up and established in its common identity, to be nourished and then to be sent out again, scattered throughout the wider society to live out and embody God's mission to his world.

It is possible for the church to make the error of focusing on preserving and building up its own life so much that we forget the horizon of the kingdom of God. Conversely, it is also possible to make the opposite error: of focusing so much on the horizon of the kingdom that we neglect those structures and areas of the life of the church which sustain us in that mission. Jesus and the apostles model a way of forming and living Christian community which has a balanced rhythm in which time is given generously to meeting together in worship and fellowship in order to be sustained in the life of loving service to which God has called us.

Transforming communities offer an additional way for this rhythm of worship and mission to be expressed in the Christian life, alongside the public gathering of the congregation Sunday by Sunday. There are certainly some who would argue that to create this additional way of coming together must therefore take away time and energy from Christian mission and Christian involvement in our wider society. How can this additional energy focused within the church be justified? The answer is in so far as this investment means a better fulfilling of the call of the whole Church to love God and our neighbour. If an attempt to establish small groups within the life of the church leads to the church becoming even more inward looking and focused on itself, then we will certainly move backwards rather than forwards. However, as our society as a whole becomes more secular, the Church as a whole will need to invest significantly more time in establishing Christian identity through small gatherings as well as public ones so that the Christian witness to life in its totality can remain both supported and distinctive. At present, the danger is that Christian life and witness is not being sustained in many different contexts. This is because Christians are largely unsupported in terms of their learning or commitment or courage or witness and inadequately initiated into the Christian life. This in turn is because their identity is being nurtured only through large gatherings in which it is impossible to form real relationships. A greater investment in these transforming communities will there-fore mean, over time, a full engagement by the whole Church with the whole of society in a genuine rhythm of worship and mission.

Roots and Resources

Jesus and the disciples

As will be apparent, the concept of transforming communities in the life of the Christian Church is not new, even though the terminology may be slightly different. The basic paradigm for small communities as the trellis and framework for the life of the church is the small community of disciples formed by Jesus whose story is told in the Gospels. Jesus dealt with multitudes yet he chose to spend time with, call, train and enable a relatively small group who were then able to carry forward God's mission.[15] This is a community which spends time in one another's company, which travels together, which embraces different individuals, which supports one another, which knows its share of conflict and which learns, grows and serves together. There is sufficient evidence from the Gospels to know that Jesus himself is sustained by these friendships and the common life.

From the earliest accounts of Jesus' ministry onwards there is, therefore, both a public and a personal aspect to the earliest Christian community. Mark's Gospel describes the beginning of Jesus' ministry as when he went into Galilee 'proclaiming the good news of God',[16] presumably in public declarations. In the very next verses we see Jesus meeting in a more personal context calling a small group of disciples to follow him. In verses 21–8 of Mark 1, the scene is again a public one as Jesus preaches in the synagogue in Capernaum. We then return to a personal and small group encounter as Jesus with-draws to the home of Simon and heals his mother-in-law before his ministry becomes public again as 'the whole city was gathered around the door'. The next morning, we see Jesus praying alone and then interacting in a small group with 'Simon and his companions' before the ministry becomes public once more. Read on into Mark's Gospel and you will find the same pattern in each chapter: we are shown a public ministry but also a more personal one, in homes, in small communities and with individuals. The same pattern is repeated in Matthew, Luke and John.

The Church of the New Testament period

You may think that this aspect of the Gospel accounts is so obvious as not to be worth mentioning. In some ways that is the case. Yet the Gospel writers mean us to take note not only of how things were for Jesus but of a pattern for the church in which there will be both public proclamation, witness and encounter in larger groups but also more personal gatherings and encounters for the Christian community for teaching, encouragement, the building of relation-ships and equipping for Christian service. As the Gospel story is traced through into Acts, we see a similar pattern emerging in the church in Jerusalem. There is a public witness as the early Christians meet in the temple and preach in open places but also smaller gatherings of little communities as the early Christians gather in one another's homes: 'Day by day, as they spent much time together in the temple, they broke bread at home and ate their food with glad and generous hearts, praising God and having the goodwill of all the people.'[17] The time of the greatest missionary effectiveness of the church was also a time in which the Christians invested hugely in establishing fellowship, relationship and identity in smaller groups as well as large, public gatherings. This pattern continues in the different centres to which the faith spreads. The pattern of early Christian assembly was, ideally, for the church to meet both publicly and in the homes of its disciples. Persecution from the Jewish communities or the Roman authorities made public assembly difficult from time to time. However, Paul looks back on his pastoral ministry in Ephesus as one of teaching 'publicly and from house to house'.[18] The church in any large city would consist of a number of smaller communities, each meeting in someone's home.[19] The pattern of worship and ministry which evolved in the early Church of mutual edification through the gifts of the whole community would only be possible in the size of group that could meet in a large home.[20]

The catechumenate

In the early centuries of Christianity, there is only limited evidence for the pattern of early Christian fellowship and a pattern of meeting together. Apart from the major centres, the numbers of Christians in any one place would not be large. The limited evidence we do have suggests a continued emphasis on personal relationship and community. The theological focus of the life of the church rests in grappling with the larger issues.

The pattern of more extended meeting together with discussion, teaching and an emphasis upon community life was certainly preserved in the catechumenate. This was the very thorough process developed from the end of the New Testament period onwards for initiating new converts into the life of faith and the Christian community and preparing them for baptism. Different models of the catechumenate began to develop in different geographical centres from an early period. However, each lays an emphasis on an extended period of initiation; of instruction separate from the main Christian community; of formation in community for at least part of the time. The early Church was preparing its members for a lifetime of costly Christian discipleship in a society in which there was almost always some degree of persecution and occasionally martyrdom to be faced.

However, in the period following the conversion of Constantine, as Christianity at last became established as the religion of the Roman Empire, the picture started to change. The mainstream life of the Church began to pay more attention to its development as an institution with larger buildings, frequent public assemblies and hierarchies of stipendiary clergy, than to the aspect of its life to be found in smaller, less formal communities. From that time onwards, wherever Christianity (or part of it) has considered itself to be the dominant religion and people have been assumed to have been Christian unless they opted out as adults, there has been no need to develop separate structures of Christian community and identity over against the wider society. The group which gathers for worship in the church building on Sundays is already a community and society, made up of families, employers and employees who live and work in the same place, friends and neighbours. There is no need to develop effective structures for initiation and mission in this context, other than for the instruction of children in the faith, because almost everyone is already part of the church. The needs of the church in this context are met by specially trained professional ministers, skilled in the offering of worship, in the instruction of children and in offering care and support in times of transition and difficulty. Mission is what happens to those beyond the boundaries of

Christendom and does not require a significant degree of involvement by the average church member.

The monastic movement

Insights, roots and resources for the life of intentional, missionary and small communities from this point onwards do not come very readily from the mainstream Church in either the East or the West.[21] Instead, we find inspiration from two sources (which often overlap). The first is from movements which emerge concerned with the renewal of the life of the Church or the restoration of values which are perceived to be lost. The second is from movements concerned with mission and particularly with mission beyond the boundaries of the Christian community. Several of these movements can be identified over the sweep of Christian history. The most influential, and the stream of Christian life which has borne the most clear witness to this aspect of our discipleship, is undoubtedly the monastic movement. The Rule of Benedict was developed to enable Christians to share and foster a common life built around a rhythm of worship and mission expressed as service of the kingdom of God. One of the driving forces for the formation of Christian communities was the perception that the wider society was becoming significantly less Christian following the decline and fall of the power of the Roman Empire. Therefore there was a need for Christians to draw together and establish alternative societies to enable a deeper devotion to Christ. The rule still has many good things to say to Christians attempting to share a common life today.[22] The monastic orders themselves had a profound impact on Western civilisation: the great cathedrals, the preservation of scholarship and classical learning, the ancient universities with their collegial system are all part of its rich legacy. These and other achievements are a testimony to how much can be achieved by Christians sharing their lives together, fostering a common identity, developing a rhythm of worship and mission and working with common purpose. The mission communities founded by the Celtic Church were centres of worship and of mission reaching out to Ireland, Scotland and northern England and remain a powerful influence on the Church in the present day.[23] Later monastic movements retain an emphasis upon Christian people coming together to enable one another in mission. The Franciscan order worked for the relief of poverty and the conversion of the Church 'from within'. The Ignatian order, during the Counter-reformation, developed a strong tradition of mission beyond the boundaries of Christendom, pioneering work which the Protestant missionary societies would develop further.

The Reformation and beyond

At the Reformation, as patterns of church life were renewed, there were clearly some attempts to encourage informal communities of Christian people to meet and study together. Luther's own home was a place for regular gatherings of Christian people and Christian conversation. The stories of each of the Reformers demonstrates the importance of relationship and Christian community, not least among those who were pioneering new developments in the life of the Church. William Beckham quotes the German Reformer, Martin Luther, as follows:

> The third kind of service (after the Latin Mass and German liturgy) should be a truly evangelical order and should not be held in a public place for all sorts of people. But those who want to be Christians in earnest and who profess the gospel with hand and mouth should sign their names and meet along in a house somewhere to pray, to read, to baptize and read the sacrament, and to do other Christian works . . .[24]

Teaching in the home was a commended, honoured and accepted pattern of Christian ministry in the Nonconformist churches and the Church of England from the Reformation onwards. It is, for example, most warmly commended by Richard Baxter, Vicar of Kidderminster from 1647 to 1661, in his classic text on ministry, *The Reformed Pastor*.[25] There is evidence throughout the seventeenth and eighteenth centuries of informal cottage meetings in the life of the Church of England, together with the more formal religious societies of different kinds which form the background to the emergence of bands and class meetings which were such an important part of Methodism.[26]

> The setting up of small Christian cells or societies within the larger Church was marked by an emphasis on fellowship, discipline, and a rootedness of Christian living in daily life. These tightly-knit 'class meetings' as they were called, so typical

of eighteenth and nineteenth century Methodism, are now rare. Many factors, spiritual, theological and sociological, have contributed to their widespread, though by no means complete, demise. There can be little doubt that the Church is the poorer for it.[27]

The Methodist Church was the first mainstream denomination to make provision for a network of smaller communities to facilitate growth in discipleship, fellowship, worship and service. Wesley's recognition that the Church was, after all, in a missionary situation in Great Britain and America, particularly among the working classes, played a vital role in this development. The Methodist pattern of deployment of all stipendiary ministers as itinerant between different congregations in a circuit is a contrast to the more settled pattern of the Church of England and other denominations and depends not only upon active lay ministry in terms of preaching but the intentional formation of community life through the network of class meetings or by other means. Christian community and formation is not dependent upon stipendiary ministers: the structure which results is based upon smaller communities not congregations. From the eighteenth century onwards such smaller communities form part of many different streams of church life in the nineteenth and twentieth centuries, normally as an 'optional extra' to membership of a congregation and attendance at Sunday worship. Very often these small communities would draw their members from a number of different churches. The tremendous expansion of the missionary societies during the nineteenth century was dependent upon the support given by small groups or societies at the level of the local church providing practical, prayer and financial support and providing the basis of teaching such that men and women would offer themselves for service overseas.

One writer has the following comment on cottage meetings in Lancashire in the mid-nineteenth century, used by all of the evangelical churches:

> According to the Lancashire and Cheshire Baptist Association such meetings served to 'call into exercise and improve the gifts of the brethren, and are thus very frequently the first introduction to ministerial and pastoral labours and usefulness'. Cottage prayer meetings offered the ordinary convert, within a

few hundred yards of his or her own home, the possibility of the sort of fellowship previously enjoyed only by the covenanted elect and they must have provided vital encouragement, especially for working-class adherents struggling to maintain their faith in an unamenable culture.[28]

The house group movement

Throughout the twentieth century, building on this tradition, house groups or fellowship groups in different forms became an established part of the life of many churches although their life ebbed and flowed somewhat. To a large extent the groups became simply a means of building up the faith and discipleship of the members or a way of managing the pastoral care of larger congregations. The emphasis on enabling mission to the whole of life and of common endeavour for the kingdom was largely lost.[29]

In the last two decades of the twentieth century and the first years of the twenty-first, two very significant movements in the world Church have begun to affect and influence the Church in the United Kingdom. Both emphasise in different ways the power of small, transforming communities as the foundation of church life.

Base ecclesial communities

The first movement is that of base ecclesial communities and originates primarily in the Roman Catholic Church in South and Central America. The theological background to the movement is that provided by liberation theology, itself a broad movement with many strands. The concept of mission which guides the communities and the movement is therefore largely that of bringing about social, economic and political change. The emphasis in the life of the groups is on empowering the members in their everyday lives. Most of the groups share a common philosophy of education based upon the pioneering work of Paulo Freire. The movement describes itself as being 'bottom-up' – an alternative to the hierarchical structures of the Roman Catholic Church.[30]

The Cell Church movement

The second movement is that of Cell Church, which originated in the Pacific Rim countries, most notably in Korea and Singapore although it has now spread right round the world. Cell Church is mainly Protestant and Pentecostal in origin although some Roman Catholic congregations have deployed its insights. The theological background is undoubtedly that of conservative evangelical theology, largely emanating from the seminaries and research institutes of the United States. Not surprisingly therefore, the concept of mission in the Cell Church movement and in individual cells focuses upon making disciples and upon church growth. There is an emphasis on equipping every member of the church to fulfil the Great Commission. As practised in Asia and as reported in other countries, the emphasis is on a top-down movement (in contrast to base ecclesial communities). In the spirit of the Methodist class meeting, there is an emphasis on the accountability of church members to one another within the cell. Within a mature cell church, the small group becomes the basic unit of the church and of church growth.[31]

Contemporary and transitional communities

A large number of other contemporary communities play their part in the resourcing and renewing of church life both through welcoming visitors for short or long periods and through the development of resources for the wider Church. Taizé and the Iona Community and other more traditional religious houses are regular places of sojourn and pilgrimage for a wide range of people who return renewed and refreshed to their places of work and worship. These communities provide rich resources for renewing worship and building up the common life. L'Arche communities have had a very significant impact on the churches in recent years, not least through the writings of Henri Nouwen[32] and Jean Vanier.[33] These communities in turn provide rich resources for any Christian wishing to explore the value and potential of life together. Established communities of welcome and hospitality such as Scargill House and Lee Abbey share in this ministry by providing the facilities needed for groups of Christians to come away from their daily circumstances and live with others for a few days and experience temporary community. The deeper relationships and insights are taken back and renew the life of the church. In a similar but different way, larger gatherings such as New Wine, Spring Harvest, Greenbelt, young people's camps and other pilgrimages and festivals are both sustained by and enrich the wider Church in its understanding of community. One diocesan bishop wrote in response to an early draft of *Transforming Communities* that 'of the parishes which are prospering, growing and vital, most, if not all, have a resource through "communities" such as Spring Harvest, Taizé, New Wine, Lee Abbey and L'Arche.'[34]

From this all too brief overview of the role which small communities have played and still play in the development of the Christian Church it is possible to make two observations. In the first place, there are significant resources upon which we can draw in thinking about this way of being church which focuses on the intentional development of small transforming communities as the basic framework for the church's life and growth. It is unlikely that any of them will provide the exact blueprint for our own situation, whether it be the form of the church in the New Testament, Methodist class meetings, the Cell Church movement or base ecclesial communities. Each is available as encouragement, as a model of different ways of shaping the life of the church and as a resource for practical help. Secondly, we have reached a point in history where the whole Church in the West must acknowledge that we have come to the end of Christendom. We all live now in a missionary context. In practice, some sections of the Church have always acknowledged that to be true: the Franciscans in the twelfth century, the Anabaptists in the sixteenth, the Methodists in the eighteenth century. In previous generations, the question may have been debatable. In the present context it is not. Therefore the denominational Churches have an urgent need to develop again small communities of Christian people which are effective as contexts for nurturing relationships, identity and mission. In the twentieth century, such small communities were desirable but not essential. In the twenty-first century such communities are now a requirement if the church is both to maintain and develop its common life.

However, before we move on to look at practical questions involved in shaping the life of the church around transforming communities, it is vital that we gain a broader and deeper understanding of what the church is and is called to be. That will be our subject in Part Three.

Which of these resources will be most important to you as you move forward?

Which do you need to get to know?

Can you think of others?

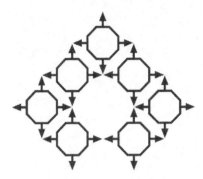

PART THREE

Nurturing the Vision: The Church in Scripture and Tradition

Introduction

We live, as we have seen, in times of significant change for the people of God. In such a time it becomes important for us to think deeply about what it means to be the church. If we neglect to do this, there is a danger that we will become discouraged (if we no longer share in success as the world sees it) or distracted from our calling and purpose by secondary issues or that we make poor, ill-informed decisions for the future. To gain fresh vision it is vital that we both understand our context but also listen carefully to our tradition, and particularly to the Scriptures. Part Three of this book is designed to help in that process.

In the story in Chapter One, the small group begins to think again about what it means to be church by reflecting together on just three passages from Acts about Christian community, mission and ministry. Another way of seeing this section of *Transforming Communities* is as providing additional material for this stage of the process in order to help us to understand our identity and our calling. I hope that this part of the book might be studied by groups as well as read by individuals. The questions at the end of each chapter could be taken as the material for four or more meetings of an existing home group, an embryo transforming community, a Deanery Pastoral Committee, a local ministry team or any group charged with nurturing the life of the church and guiding its future. You may also find them helpful in some circumstances for linking this material with a short series of Sunday sermons on the nature of the church.

There is an enormous range of published material on the nature and life of the church and I have referred to some of this in the notes and in the bibliography at the back of the book for students and others who would like to explore the ideas further. More is being published all the time. Much of this published material is helpful but

I have found in reading it that most falls into one of two categories. The first is very detailed and careful study of ecclesiology (the term for the theology of the church) largely, in recent years, from the perspective of the ecumenical movement. Different denominations have developed over time a range of understandings both of their own Church and of other Churches. In order to move forward in dialogue and towards greater unity it is very important to develop a common language. This has begun to happen in different ways over the last forty years and is an important achievement. However, I have found it hard to make real connections between writing about the Church undertaken for this purpose and the life of a local congregation. The ecumenical writings can seem somewhat remote and (dare I say it?) dull. The second kind of literature is a range of more popular level writing on how to guide and to be a local church in different settings. Some of this literature is surveyed in Chapter Four. This kind of writing about the church tends to be very practical (which is good and important) but seems to neglect the vital task of nurturing our understanding of what the church is and is called to be. Part Three attempts to provide a bridge between these two kinds of books and between the practical suggestions in the rest of the book and the Christian tradition.

The Christian church has been reflecting on its own life for almost two thousand years. No single book (or section of a book) can do justice to the whole of that tradition. I have therefore had to be selective: seeking to draw out those parts of an understanding of the church which seem to me to be the most important for our present time. What follows is not intended to be a complete definition of what it means to be church but simply a description to help others see more fully and more clearly and therefore to be refreshed, renewed and envisioned in their journey. Whether you are reading this as an individual or with a group, there may be things you want to add to the understanding of church which is written here; perspectives you want to change; lines of thought you may want to take further. The purpose of this section of the book is to provoke exactly that kind of reflection rather than to provide the last word on the subject.

At the beginning of Tolkien's epic fantasy, *The Lord of the Rings*, the hobbits who are at the centre of the story, perceive Gandalf the wizard as an elderly conjuror, respected for his ability to blow wonderful smoke rings and create the most marvellous fireworks. As the journey unfolds, the hobbits gradually learn more and more about the history, ability and importance of this most wonderful character through his actions and stories and as they see him through the eyes of others who have known him longer. It is not until the very last pages of the book that the full truth about Gandalf is made known. In a similar way, for most of us, our first encounter with the church is often very unimpressive: a small gathering of Christian people, perhaps mainly elderly, seemingly ignored by the wider world, all too often imperfect, divided and stumbling in its worship and witness.

According to C.S. Lewis, the experienced devil Screwtape writes to the young tempter Wormwood, shortly after Wormwood's 'patient' has become a Christian:

> One of our great allies at present is the Church itself. Do not misunderstand me. I do not mean the Church as we see her spread through all time and space and rooted in eternity, terrible as an army with banners. That, I confess, is a spectacle which makes our boldest tempters uneasy. But fortunately it is quite invisible to these humans. All your patient sees is the half-finished, sham Gothic erection on the new building estate. When he goes inside, he sees the local grocer with rather an oily expression on his face bustling up to offer him one shiny little book containing a liturgy which neither of them understands, and one shabby little book containing corrupt texts of a number of religious lyrics, mostly bad and in very small print. When he gets to his pew and looks round him he sees just that selection of his neighbours whom he has hitherto avoided.[1]

As we go on in our journey, we need the opportunity to learn more about this elderly lady[2] for, like many older people, there is rather more to her than meets the eye.

I have chosen here to describe the church through four different relationships: with God, with herself, with the world and with time. Enjoy the journey!

7

The Called Community: The Church in Relationship with God

But you are a chosen race, a royal priesthood, a holy nation, God's own people, in order that you may proclaim the mighty acts of him who called you out of darkness into his marvellous light. Once you were not a people, but now you are God's people; once you had not received mercy, but now you have received mercy.[1]

The author of 1 Peter writes to encourage a young, minority church scattered throughout the known world which is convinced that, from a human perspective, it is unlikely to survive. The numbers of people who form this church are not large compared to the society around them. They are dispersed across whole continents and held together by a handful of imperfect leaders with little formal structure. They suffer all kinds of grief and trials,[2] internal pressure to fragment and divide as well as a host of practical problems.

Where does any writer begin to unite and to encourage such a community? The book of 1 Peter begins with the reminder that the life of the church originates in the call of God. The word used in the New Testament for 'church' is *ekklesia*, which simply means 'called out'.[3] In the New Testament, of course, the word 'church' is never used to describe a building but describes a particular group of people. The church is the community that God has created by calling men and women into relationship with himself and with one another. The Christian church has never believed that we are simply a human organisation and society invented by the early Christians. The church would not exist at all unless God himself had called us into being and sustained us by his presence.

The People of God

God's call which forms community does not begin with Jesus but is deeply rooted in the Old Testament story. The story of God taking a people for himself and calling them out from the world to share in his mission to the world begins with the call of Abram: 'Go from your country, your kindred and your father's house to the land that I will show you.'[4] This first community called into being by God's grace is centred around a single family. The purpose of God's call from the very beginning is not for the blessing of Abram and his family alone but in order to be a community such that 'all the people on earth will be blessed through you'.[5]

In time this single extended family become a much larger nation. The sense of God's call and choosing of Israel as his own people is immeasurably strengthened and deepened through the experience of the exodus from Egypt. God hears the cry of those who were enslaved and, through a series of miracles, leads them out of slavery to freedom in the Promised Land. The promise of freedom is accompanied by a promise that Israel will be the people of God:

> 'I will take you as my people and I will be your God. You shall know that I am the Lord your God who has freed you from the burdens of the Egyptians.'[6]

> For ask now about former ages, long before your own, ever since the day that God created human beings on the earth; ask from one end of heaven to the other: has anything so great as this ever happened or has its like ever been heard of? Has any people ever heard the voice of a god speaking out of a fire, as you have heard, and lived? Or has any god ever attempted to go and take a nation for himself from the midst of another nation, by trials, by signs and wonders, by war, by a mighty hand and

outstretched arm, and by terrifying displays of power, as the Lord your God did for you in Egypt before your very eyes?[7]

The prophets and psalmists of the Old Testament celebrate over and over again the great miracle of salvation by which Israel becomes a free nation, chosen and set aside for God's own purpose. Yet there are two immense struggles within the nation of Israel concerning this call to be the people of God. One looks inward, the other outward. The first concerns Israel's failure, in the eyes of her own prophets, to respond and live up to the ideal of becoming God's holy people. Reminding one another of salvation in history is not enough. There is a need for a deeper transformation and more radical change. In the last analysis, this can only come about through the grace of God working in the lives of his people. The prophets look forward to God recalling and restoring Israel through a deep and continual experience of forgiveness and change:

> The days are surely coming, says the Lord, when I will make a new covenant with the house of Israel and the house of Judah. It will not be like the covenant that I made with their ancestors when I took them by the hand to bring them out of the land of Egypt – a covenant that they broke, though I was their husband, says the Lord. But this is the covenant that I will make with the house of Israel after those days, says the Lord: I will put my law within them, and I will write it on their hearts; and I will be their God, and they shall be my people. No longer shall they teach one another, or say to one another, 'Know the Lord', for they shall all know me, from the least of them to the greatest, says the Lord; for I will forgive their iniquity, and remember their sin no more.[8]

The second struggle is to keep in mind the purpose of Israel's calling to be God's people *for the sake of the whole world*. There is a continual temptation for the nation to see itself as special for its own sake and because of its own virtue rather than called by grace for the sake of God's mission. A series of challenges ring out throughout Israel's history reminding God's people that God's concern is for the whole of creation and for all the nations: Israel's election is for a purpose.[9] That purpose is the restoring of God's order and God's kingdom among the nations and in the whole of human society. This is a much wider vision than calling all the nations of the earth to worship the God of Israel in Jerusalem (although that certainly forms part of Israel's vocation). The vision embraces the establishing of God's justice and order throughout the whole of human society and, as a result, the transformation even of the natural order.

Israel is unable in her own strength to live up to God's call and to fulfil God's mission. For that reason, the books of the Old Testament look forward to the time when God's servant will come. This servant of God, the Messiah, will call to God a new missionary community not only from Israel but from the nations. The Spirit of God will be poured out on God's called community to help them to grow in holiness and to fulfil God's mission.

> 'Then afterwards I will pour out my spirit on all flesh: your sons and your daughters shall prophesy, your old men shall dream dreams, and your young men shall see visions. Even on the male and female slaves, in those days, I will pour out my spirit.'[10]

The Christian Church needs to understand and relearn in every generation that God's call of a people to himself does not begin with Jesus or the Acts of the Apostles but with Abraham. We also need to understand that God's call for the Church to be the people of God from every nation does not replace or supersede God's call to the Jews. God does not abandon those whom he has called and God has not abandoned his ancient people. Paul uses the picture of the people of God as being like an ancient olive tree. The Church has been grafted in like new shoots to share in God's grace:

> But if some of the branches were broken off, and you, a wild olive shoot, were grafted in their place, to share the rich root of the olive tree, do not vaunt yourselves over the branches. If you do vaunt yourselves, remember that it is not you that support the root, but the root that supports you.[11]

The First Disciples

The motif of the call of God shaping a community for mission is in evidence, as we have seen, from the very first pages of the Gospel accounts of the coming of God's Son. Although Jesus welcomes and cares for everyone who comes to him from individuals to great crowds, all the Gospels tell us that he calls out particular individuals to leave everything and to follow him. As is clear from numerous passages, the vocation of the disciples is not only to a series of individual relationships with Jesus but to life in a missionary community. They are in relationship with one another in times of learning, leisure, fellowship and support, and in mission. The stories of Peter and Andrew, James and John and others are told in great detail not only for historical interest but because they are models and patterns of the way in which God calls people in every generation to discipleship and service.[12] The Book of Acts has new stories of call and conversion which build a bridge between the Gospel encounters and our experiences today. It would, perhaps, be possible to tell the story of the ministry, death and resurrection of Jesus without mentioning the disciples at all or to see them as playing a minor supportive role in the drama. This is not what we find in the four Evangelists. The initial action of Jesus' ministry, according to Mark, is the call of the first disciples into a small community.[13] From the very beginning, Jesus is not only supported by this group but gives time to teaching and dialogue with them. By the third chapter of Mark's Gospel, twelve are appointed to be apostles 'to be with him, and to be sent out to proclaim the message'.[14]

After this point, the group of disciples is almost always present with Jesus. They are the prototype Christian community. But it is vital to note that each one is present because, one by one, they have heard and responded to the call of Christ. We are told some of these call stories in great detail. Simon Peter is amazed because of an enormous catch of fish.[15] Matthew abandons his work as a tax collector.[16] Other call stories are left to our imagination. But the Gospels make clear that these disciples have not simply *chosen* to come and follow the one they will learn to know as Christ. This is more than a good idea or a passing inclination. Nor are the disciples present simply because they have been *invited* as guests to a banquet. A call is much stronger than an invitation because it involves leaving everything behind. The disciples respond to grace and are formed into a community because Jesus called them. They left everything to follow him.

There has been considerable debate throughout Christian history about the relationship between this early community of disciples

113

and the Christian church. It is certainly important to note, as I have already mentioned, that the word 'church' (*ekklesia*) only appears twice in the Gospels. In Matthew we read first that Peter is called to be the rock upon which, Jesus says, 'I will build my church'[17] and then, two chapters later, we are told how differences are to be resolved in the community of believers: 'If the member refuses to listen to them, tell it to the church'.[18] Some theologians have argued that it was not Jesus' intention to call a community into being at all. The New Testament scholar A. Loisy wrote many years ago that 'Jesus proclaimed the kingdom of God, and what came was the Church.'[19]

Jesus did indeed come proclaiming God's kingdom. Yet as part of the proclamation and fulfilment of that kingdom and the means to its furtherance, he clearly calls into being this small community of disciples which is to become, after his resurrection, the first Christian community. A significant amount of space is given over to this group in each of the Gospels and the lessons which are learned by the disciples are not recorded for historical interest but are clearly intended as lessons for the church. The group is formed by travelling together, through shared meals and shared experiences, through teaching and learning, question and answer, through prayer and worship, through success and also by failure, in poverty and in plenty. We see the words in Mark's Gospel fulfilled as the disciples are both with Jesus and sent out by him to share in the mission to the communities around. They learn together about God's nature and mission, about authority and power, about shared priorities, about preaching and healing, about signs and wonders and the values of the kingdom. Together they experience both the exhilaration of the mountain-tops and the exhaustion of the valleys. They reflect with Jesus on the cost of discipleship, on the difficult road before them, on suffering and, ultimately, death and resurrection. Jesus himself describes this little community as closer than a natural human family.[20] The twelve and the wider group of about 120 who are together after the resurrection (according to Luke) become part of a transforming community: they themselves are changed dramatically by their encounters with Jesus and with one another. Together, by the grace of God, they go on to transform the entire world.

This transforming community comes into being because of God's call in Christ. Like the people of God of old, the new community shares a sense of being redeemed, of being saved by God from slavery. The language of the Exodus is taken up into the language of the church's self-understanding.[21] Each member of the community and the Church as a whole is made new through the powerful and transformative event of the death and resurrection of Jesus which gives a Gospel shape to the life of the people of God. The new covenant is made possible only because of the death of Christ. A new meal for the new community takes the place of the Passover. The Holy Spirit is given to the new community so that the people will themselves grow in holiness[22] and be equipped and strengthened to share in God's mission.[23]

Called to Be with Him and to Be Sent Out

The self-understanding of the people of God which develops in the New Testament grows up from these roots. The concepts of God's grace and call are fundamental both for individuals and for the community as a whole. The Christian community is called to be and to become the people of God in fulfilment of Scripture; redeemed through the death and resurrection of Christ and sanctified and empowered for mission by the Spirit. All of these elements are incorporated into the great sacrament of baptism.

This calling to the Christian community is a vocation to the rhythm of worship and mission which is so beautifully caught by Mark's intentional description of the purpose of the calling of the first disciples: to be with him and to be sent out. The rhythm is caught, as we have seen, in Jesus' answer to the question as to what is the greatest commandment:[24] love of God and love of others: worship and mission. Over and over again we are reminded throughout the New Testament that the church is called to be a people dedicated to God's praise: from the picture of worship which begins and ends the Gospel of Luke; to the centrality of worship in the life of the early Church in Acts; in the beautiful passage at the beginning of Ephesians in which we are called 'to the praise of his glory';[25] to the passage from 1 Peter at the head of this chapter: 'But you are a chosen race, a royal priesthood, a holy nation, God's own people, in order that you may proclaim the mighty acts of him who called you out of darkness into his marvellous light.'[26] The final book of the New Testament is centred around and calls us towards, as we shall see, a picture of the saints, God's holy people, at worship in heaven, celebrating the presence of God in the whole of life:

> I saw no temple in the city, for its temple is the Lord God the Almighty and the Lamb. And the city has no need of sun or moon to shine on it, for the glory of God is its light and its lamp is the Lamb.[27]

Yet the early Christians never limit their call to community and worship alone. The vocation to be the people of God means that the church is called to share in the mission of God to the whole of society and the whole of creation. Attention is given to the proper ordering of their own communities, but this is always set within the context of the right ordering of the whole of society and structured so as to enable that mission. The church has a role to fulfil in God's mission through its proclamation, through its common life and through challenging society. In the teaching of Jesus in the Sermon on the Mount it is clear that the church must not see its own life as an end in itself but as fulfilling God's greater purpose for the whole world:

> 'You are the salt of the earth; but if salt has lost its taste, how can its saltiness be restored? It is no longer good for anything but is thrown out and trampled under foot. You are the light of the world. A city built on a hill cannot be hid. No-one after lighting a lamp puts it under the basket but on the lamp stand and it gives light to all in the house.'[28]

In Romans 8, as we shall see, the church has a part to play in the purposes of God not only for humanity but for all of creation: 'For the creation waits with eager longing for the revealing of the children of God'.[29]

The Bride of Christ

So, then, the church is no mere human society according to Christian teaching. God is intimately involved in the life of this community as Father, Son and Holy Spirit: calling the church into being; redeeming its members; sustaining them in both discipleship and mission. This sense of deep and sacrificial love between the Lord and his Church is caught boldly and tenderly in the New Testament picture of the Church as the Bride of Christ. The image builds upon the powerful metaphors in the Old Testament of God's love for Israel being that of a faithful husband for a faithless wife.[30] There are allusions in Jesus' parables to the coming of the kingdom resembling a wedding feast or banquet[31] and Jesus describes himself as the bridegroom to the disciples of John the Baptist. Paul uses the picture of marriage explicitly to refer to the intimate relationship of love between Christ and the Church. Writing to the Corinthian church he takes the position of a matchmaker: 'I feel a divine jealousy for you, for I promised you in marriage to one husband, to present you as a chaste virgin to Christ.'[32] The image is taken up in the Book of Revelation in the great picture of the marriage feast of the Lamb.[33] The Christian tradition then, from an early date, begins to read the picture backwards into other Old Testament texts about marriage, particularly the wedding song of Psalm 45 and the Song of Songs. These great pictures of marriage and love are applied to the devotion and love between Christ and his Bride and through that image to the love between Christ and the believer.[34] Again, this is no ordinary community. The church is not only called, redeemed and made holy by God but is loved by God, passionately, personally and intimately, caught up and invited to be united with God himself for all eternity.

Trinity and Communion

What is this life of God into which the church is called, invited and caught up? The end point of Christian reflection on the nature of God is the understanding of the Trinity, God as one yet three persons: Father, Son and Holy Spirit. In recent decades there has been something of a rediscovery of the wonder of seeing and appreciating God in this way and much of the Church has begun to contemplate fresh aspects of the nature of God as three persons in an interrelationship of love.[35] This recovery of trinitarian theology has had a profound and attractive impact upon ecumenical discussions about the nature of the church. Its most popular representation is in the orthodox icon ascribed to the painter Rublev, showing the

Father, Son and Holy Spirit as the angels visiting Abraham at the oaks of Mamre. The Church has moved away from seeing the Trinity as an ordered progression from the Father to the Son to the Spirit to seeing the Trinity as a community of love. The way is clear, therefore, to see the church much more as an open community reflecting the nature of God himself. We move from seeing the church as a hierarchy of different groups (bishops, clergy and laity) to an open and mutually supportive community which itself shares in communion with the Trinity. This in turn has led to a profoundly different view of the place of the ordained ministry within the life of this community.[36]

Communion and Sacrament

All of these strands which make up the church's own understanding of itself in relationship to God are taken up into the Eucharist, the great sacrament of the new covenant. Here, as the church assembles together for worship on the Lord's day, we are reminded of the grace of God in creation, in redemption through the death and resurrection of Jesus, and in the gift of the Spirit.[37] We hear again in the words of the service and especially the words of Scripture, God's call to come and follow and to be part of this new community. We are invited to come and to share together in the body and blood of Christ present through faith in the bread and wine: an effective sign both of the death and resurrection of Christ for our sake but also of our own intimate communion with God and his presence in the life of the believer.[38]

The Grace of God and the Shape of the Church

How should all of this part of our understanding of the church affect the way we shape its life? The images and themes discussed in this chapter indicate, first and foremost, that the Church as a whole and each community of believers are infinitely precious to God as a bride is dear to her husband. Any group planning for and shaping the life of the church in one place or a wider area need, in the words of the ordinal, to 'remember always with thanksgiving that the treasure . . .

entrusted to you is Christ's own flock, bought through the shedding of his blood on the cross. The Church and congregation ... whom you serve are one with him; they are his body'.[39] This is more than a simply human community. This is God's society. By extension, care needs to be taken, therefore, of each member of the church, because of the great love and esteem in which each is held by God. Secondly, we need to be mindful that this is a community called into being by the grace of God, for the purpose of God and is, in the final analysis, nurtured and sustained by God. There is a great deal of difference between attempting to shape the life of the church as a semi-failing institution under financial or practical pressures from society around us, on the one hand, and finding a way forward with God for the people of God, on the other. Third, this is a community which is called to reflect the nature of God, three persons in community. We seek to move therefore in a direction which builds community, relationship, a valuing of koinonia, fellowship with one another and with God. Fourthly and finally, God calls the church to this dynamic rhythm of worship and mission to the whole world and in the whole of our lives. The structures we develop therefore need to enhance and support this rhythm, enabling the whole people of God to live out their vocation.

There is no single 'right' way of shaping and directing the life of the church. Some ways will be appropriate in one culture and context, others in another. However, shaping the life of the church around small transforming communities in our own generation is certainly consistent with holding the church and all its members as precious to God since within a smaller community each person is valued; no one is overlooked or forgotten. It is consistent with believing that God is at work renewing and sustaining this community for the continual renewal of the whole of society: one of the great gaps in Western society is the lack of relationship and community within our structures.[40] Developing small missionary communities can be a vital way of sustaining each member of the church in their discipleship and in living out the great rhythm of worship and of mission.

Tell the story of how God called you as a Christian to the church you are part of (and to this group).

How were the first disciples called into a community? What lessons can we learn for the church today?

Do you find it helpful to think of God the Holy Trinity as an open communion of love and as a pattern for the church?

How can you develop the patterns of relating in your own church to enable the whole congregation to live out the rhythm of worship and mission?

8

Members of One Body: The Church in Relation to Herself

We are the body of Christ.
In the one Spirit we were all baptised into one body.
Let us then pursue all that makes for peace
And builds up our common life.[1]

God has called the church into existence by his love. The church is called in turn to love God in worship and in Christian service: to witness to the nature of God, share in the mission of God and reflect the likeness of God within the world. However, this calling is always to relationships with others as well as friendship with God. The relationships begin from the very personal: how three people in a meeting or small group behave towards one another. They extend to the relationships between different kinds of people in the same church (men and women; the old and the young; rich and poor; those of different races; new members and the more established; those exercising public ministry and those who do not). From there, these relationships embrace the way in which the local church is connected to the wider Christian community: to its own denomination through a variety of relationships; to churches of different denominations in the area. How is a congregation in Birmingham joined with one in Korea or Chile? How are the great Christian traditions connected to one another? Finally, how is the visible

Church here on earth connected with the Church down the ages and the saints in heaven?

From the earliest days of the Christian community, according to the New Testament, Christians have therefore needed to think carefully not only about the church's relationships with God but about the way in which Christians relate to one another within God's new society. Very often, individual Christians in our churches do not appear to be very well 'connected': they are held within a particular congregation by a series of very tenuous links (perhaps some casual acquaintances or getting to know a particular minister). When a significant life change or crisis happens, or the minister moves on, the connections of Christian fellowship are simply not strong enough to hold the person within the community. How can we guide and grow the life of the local church in such a way that these connections are continually strengthened and developed?

Christian Connections in the Four Gospels

Mark

Once again, the pattern for the church is laid by the Gospel accounts of the relationships between the disciples which are recorded because they have things to teach Christians in every generation. The four Gospels give increasing attention to the issue in the order in which they came to be written. In Mark, the earliest Gospel, Jesus teaches about unity,[2] affirms that the bonds between the disciples are as close as the bonds between a natural family[3] and deals on two occasions with the difficult issues of authority and service within the group.[4] It is generally acknowledged that the Gospel of Mark was written for a community which expected the imminent return of Christ: not a great deal of attention is given, therefore, to the ordering of the life of the people of God.

Matthew

Matthew's Gospel builds on Mark's account and includes all of the passages mentioned above. However, Matthew develops the theme of relationships within the new community further, particularly in the five great collections of Jesus' teaching which are interspersed through the Gospel.[5] Matthew is writing for a Christian community which has realised that there may be some time before Christ's return and is beginning to develop its own code of ethics and behaviour which marks it out from the rest of society and from the Jewish community from which the church sprang. The Sermon on the Mount gives instructions for this new community on such matters as swearing oaths, adultery, divorce, the treatment of friends and enemies, and private and public prayer. In Matthew 16, Peter receives the following instruction:

> 'And I tell you, you are Peter, and on this rock I will build my church, and the gates of Hades will not prevail against it. I will give you the keys of the kingdom of heaven, and whatever you bind on earth will be bound in heaven, and whatever you loose on earth will be loosed in heaven.'[6]

At the very least we are able to say the following about the church of Matthew's day: Jesus is concerned to build this new community; it has a spiritual existence and identity founded on the apostles; authority is given to it to determine its own boundaries and settle questions of ethics and conduct.

In Chapter 18 of the Gospel, as we have seen, there is explicit reference to conduct within the church. The disciples are taught the severity of causing another Christian to sin[7] and how to deal, in turn, with a fellow Christian who causes offence:

> 'If another member of the church sins against you, go and point out the fault when the two of you are alone. If the member listens to you, you have regained that one. But if you are not listened to, take one or two others along with you, so that every word may be confirmed by the evidence of two or three witnesses. If the member refuses to listen to them, tell it to the church; and if the offender refuses to listen even to the church, let such a one be to you as a Gentile and a tax collector.'[8]

The point of this passage and the one which follows is that an offence between two Christian people causes a rift not only between two individuals but within the Christian community. The whole community may therefore need to be involved in its resolution and healing. This issue raises, in turn, the question of forgiveness within the Christian community in Peter's famous question: '"Lord, if another member of the church sins against me, how often should I forgive? As many as seven times?" Jesus said to him, "Not seven times, but I tell you, seventy-seven times."[9] The question is, of course, partly about personal relationships and partly about church discipline: the early Christian community faced the question of how often a believer should be restored to fellowship after falling away. However, the question also reveals something about the depth of relationships which were experienced within it. Superficial relationships in which we simply nod to one another on a Sunday morning or exchange pleasantries, seldom cause offence or require forgiveness. The kind of Christian community envisaged by Matthew is one in which relationships are deep and real enough to demand the regular forgiveness which is essential in close families. This, in turn, implies a way of building Christian community which allows and enables relationships to grow to that point.

Luke-Acts

If Matthew gives teaching about the church through the words of Jesus, Luke tells us about the way the early Christians grappled with their relationships with one another through his stories, particularly in the Book of Acts. The Gospel of Luke contains similar material to Mark and Matthew in that Luke also records the disputes about greatness, the familial bonds between the disciples and, to some degree, portrays the ethics of the new community. Luke can be seen as extending the teaching of the other synoptic Gospels on hospitality and table fellowship both within the Christian community and beyond it.[10] He also says a very great deal about the mission of the disciples in the Gospels, as we shall see. However, most of Luke's teaching about relationships within the community is set, understandably, in his account of the early days of the church in Acts. After the death of Jesus, the small community of the disciples becomes the focus of Luke's story in the final chapter of the Gospel and the early chapters of Acts.[11] We read of the way in which this early community reached decisions about ministry[12] and of the promised gift of the Spirit at Pentecost. In several passages in the early chapters, as we have seen, Luke paints a picture of these first Christian communities as a guide and inspiration for the church in every age:

They devoted themselves to the apostles' teaching and fellow-ship, to the breaking of bread and the prayers. Awe came upon everyone, because many wonders and signs were being done by the apostles. All who believed were together and had all things in common: they would sell their possessions and goods and distribute the proceeds to all, as any had need. Day by day, as they spent much time together in the temple, they broke bread at home, and ate their food with glad and generous hearts, praising God and having the goodwill of all the people. And day by day the Lord added to their number those who were being saved.[13]

Now the whole group of those who believed were of one heart and soul and no one claimed private ownership of any posses-sions, but everything they owned was held in common. With great power, the apostles gave their testimony to the resurrec-tion of the Lord Jesus, and great grace was upon them all. There was not a needy person among them, for as many as owned land and houses sold them and brought the proceeds of what was sold. They laid it at the apostles' feet and it was distributed to each as any had need.[14]

Luke makes clear connections in the early chapters of Acts between the internal dynamics of the Christian community and its effective-ness in mission. In Acts 2:1 we are told that the Christians are 'all together in one place' when the Spirit is given, following the instruc-tions of the risen Christ. In Acts 2:42-7 Luke enables us to see a clear connection between the quality of life of the first Christians and the time they spent together and the observation that 'day by day the Lord added to their number those who were being saved'. In Acts 4:32-5, a similar connection is made between the unity of the church (unity of heart, soul and physical possessions) and the great power with which the apostles give their testimony to the resurrection of the Lord Jesus. In this instance at least, developing genuine Christian community and depth of fellowship does not detract from Christian mission but goes hand in hand with the effective communication of the gospel.

The picture of the church in the rest of Acts builds on the impression given in the early chapters. We learn how the early

Church deals with the expanding need for Christian ministry as the community grows.[15] We see small household communities established through the missionary journeys of Paul. These communities are characterised by the same close bonds of fellowship, the same gift of the Spirit and the same energy for mission as the original Jerusalem community.[16] We see, in particular, the way in which the early Church struggles to maintain its unity, as the question first of how to include the Gentile Christians is overcome and, thereafter, how Jewish and Gentile Christians share fellowship together in the same community. We see through the continual travels of the apostles how, in practice, the links between the early communities were established and maintained. As several writers have observed, Luke is extremely careful and deliberate in his use of terms for 'church' and 'ministry', including the term *ekklesia*,[17] yet the picture he gives of the early Christian communities is one in which members of the household churches are in close relationship with one another, in which disputes are sorted out honestly in order not to fracture the unity of the church, and in which the different communities in different places see themselves as part of a single society spreading throughout the world.

John

The fourth Gospel follows the pattern of Matthew, but to a greater degree, in giving extended instructions to the community of believers through the reported words and, in one case, the actions of Jesus. The discourse on Jesus as the good shepherd uses the image of the flock for the Christian community, echoing the synoptic Gospels and the Epistles. The emphasis here and elsewhere in John is on the unity of the Christian Church throughout the world: 'I have other sheep that do not belong to this fold. I must bring them also, and they will listen to my voice. So there will be one flock, one shepherd.'[18]

In the account of the foot washing which sets the scene for the last discourses in John's Gospel, Jesus sets the disciples an example for all time in their personal relationships with one another: 'So if I, your Lord and Teacher, have washed your feet, you also ought to wash one another's feet. For I have set you an example that you also should do as I have done to you.'[19] This passage is in turn followed by the first of two instructions to love one another. Again, as in Luke, the quality of relationships within the Christian community is an effective means of witness and mission to the world: 'I give you a new commandment, that you love one another. Just as I have loved you, you also should love one another. By this, everyone will know that you are my disciples, if you have love for one another.'[20]

These themes of Jesus' ongoing care for the church, his concern for unity and love between the believers and witness to the world, all come together in Jesus' great prayer for his disciples in John 17. The relationship between each believer and God creates in itself a union between the disciples which is a powerful sign to the world. This saying is not only for the first generation of disciples but for every generation:

> 'I ask not only on behalf of these, but also on behalf of those who will believe in me through their word, that they may all be one. As you, Father, are in me and I am in you, may they also be in us so that the world may believe that you have sent me. The glory that you have given me, I have given them, so that they may be one, I in them and you in me, that they may become completely one, so that the world may know that you have sent me and have loved them, even as you have loved me.'[21]

The Body of Christ

The image in the Epistles

The apostle Paul grapples with questions of relationships, connection, service and mission through the great, rich and influential image he develops of the Church as the Body of Christ. The image is developed in four of the Epistles: Romans, 1 Corinthians, Colossians and Ephesians.[22] Unlike the great image of the bride, it has no obvious Old Testament antecedents. One of the most recent and very thorough discussions of the picture traces its roots to the need the Church felt to describe a new community and society which was open to people of every race, both Jews and Gentiles, but which could not be defined by the boundaries of race or geography. The picture has probably been borrowed from contemporary historical literature and is a metaphor for unity in diversity within the secular state.[23]

In Romans and 1 Corinthians, Paul's concern is primarily to reflect upon unity and diversity within the local context to which he is writing, encouraging mutual respect and co-operation, and teaching about the gifts given by God to each part of the church. The Epistles envisage a church context which is small enough for each person's gifts to be known, recognised and used in a variety of ways. Using gifts in this way is a significant part of belonging, of worship and of Christian growth.

> Now you are the body of Christ, and each of you is a part of it.[24]

> Just as each of us has one body with many members, and these members do not all have the same function, so in Christ we who are many form one body, and each member belongs to all the others. We have different gifts according to the grace given to us ...[25]

In Colossians and Ephesians the picture is taken a stage further. Here the church in focus is not only the local but also the universal Church throughout the world, of which Christ is the head. It is in Christ and as part of the Body of Christ that different manifestations of the local church are able to relate to one another and fulfil God's purpose within creation.

> And [Christ] is the head of the body, the church; he is the beginning and the firstborn from among the dead ...[26]

> And God placed all things under his feet and appointed him to be head over everything for the church, which is his body, the fulness of him who fills everything in every way.[27]

> There is one body and one Spirit – just as you were called to one hope when you were called – one Lord, one faith, one baptism, one God and Father of all, who is over all and through all and in all.[28]

In this passage, the image of the body is used first of the whole Church throughout the world ('one body'). The concept is then used in a very similar way to Romans and 1 Corinthians to describe the diversity of gifts spread throughout the Church, some of which are deployed locally and others across the whole Body:

to prepare God's people for works of service, so that the body of Christ may be built up until we all reach unity in the faith and in the knowledge of the Son of God and become mature, attaining to the whole measure of the fulness of Christ.[29]

From him the whole body, joined and held together by every supporting ligament, grows and builds itself up in love as each part does its work.[30]

The second half of the Epistle, especially chapters 4 and 5, unpack something of what it means to build one another up (and therefore to build up the Body of Christ in this way). Again, it is assumed that Christians will be in some kind of relationship with one another, connected to one another in a deeper way than is expressed simply by being in the same building once a week and on nodding terms. To build up the Body of Christ means to give time intentionally to relationships within that Body.

A member of the Body

The concept of 'member' and of 'membership' of the church is, of course, part of this image of the body. The word 'member' derives from the Latin word *membrum* which means 'a limb or part of the body'. The word is, of course, used in a much weaker sense in modern English. When we speak of being a member of the Labour Party or the Rotary Club or a health club, we are describing quite a weak kind of belonging. The person may be aligning themselves with the views of an organisation, probably pays a subscription of some kind and, in many cases, will expect something in return for whatever is given in terms of influence or services. I suspect many people view their 'membership' of the church in similar terms. Even so, in some church circles, it is unfashionable to talk about 'membership' at all as if the term is not a very theological one.

However, in Christian theology, being a member (or limb) of the Body of Christ is a very appropriate concept drawn straight from the pages of the New Testament. The word describes a very strong and close way of belonging. It is, in fact, hard to find a closer expression of belonging. Members are physically joined to one another and physically part of one another. 'If one member suffers, all suffer together with it; if one member is honoured, all rejoice together with it';[31] 'Rejoice with those who rejoice, weep with those who weep. Live in harmony with one another'.[32] It is a way of belonging which is part of the gift, grace and responsibility of being part of God's Church. It is also a way of belonging which needs to be nurtured by patterns of association and fellowship within the community. Belonging and exercising a ministry in such a way that the whole Body is built up does not happen automatically. Yet the Body will not be built up and grow unless its members become involved. This kind of belonging therefore calls, again, for patterns of close association between Christians, knowledge of one another and genuine Christian fellowship. If the prevailing structures of church and society are such that this aspect of the church is not being nurtured, as is presently the case in many different contexts, then intentional and positive action must be taken to enable the Body of Christ to be the Body of Christ through the building of small, transforming communities.

The broken Body

The picture of the Church as the Body of Christ has been important in many strands of the Christian tradition from the time of the New Testament to the present. The image remains one of unity, both the unity of the whole Body of Christ throughout the world and the unity of particular congregations.[33] In time, of course, the Church of Christ throughout the world began to fracture and the unity of the Body is broken. Christian theologians pay more attention to what gives a particular branch of the Church the right to be considered a true Church (or even *the* true Church). The different denominations evolve different patterns of church government, membership and maintaining associational networks of congregations. Over the last two centuries there have been renewed attempts at ecumenical dialogue: helping the Church to restore the image of Christ through the healing of the wounds within the Body. This ecumenical dialogue has produced a great deal of new thinking on how we understand the Church.

To a large extent, these dialogues and questions lie outside the scope of this book. Even to describe them adequately would take a separate chapter. However, it is vital to note two very significant concerns which have been part of the church thinking about the church from the time of the New Testament until the present day and are both contained within the image of the Body of Christ.

The first is an overall concern for the fundamental unity of all Christian people throughout the world and for the Church on earth with the Church in history and eternity. This great truth is contained in the credal statement that we believe in the one, holy catholic and apostolic Church.[34] Any local church needs to be conscious of this unity and concerned to both express it and build it through reaching out to other Christian communities locally, nationally and internationally, building a web of relationships across the Body of Christ.

Secondly, each local congregation needs to be conscious of the wider picture in such a way as to avoid congregationalism: falling into the trap of allowing Christian concern for the Church to begin and end with the small community of Christians to which we belong. Even denominational and connexional churches can fall prey to this temptation. Our whole world shrinks to what is happening and what can be accomplished in our own corner of the vineyard. Our vision of Church must always be greater than the local. In the Church of England this great truth is expressed and maintained through the diocese and the bishop being a primary unit of belonging and oversight alongside the parish. Normally, this truth is underlined very powerfully by Anglican congregations contributing an agreed sum or share to the diocesan budget and the dioceses contributing in their turn to a national budget so that the expenses of stipendiary ministry are divided.

One image among many

The picture of the Church as the Body of Christ is a powerful image for describing the degree of connection between individuals and between congregations. It has formed a significant part of current Church of England reflection upon the ordering of our common life.[35] As the Archbishop of York and others have recently pointed out, however, we need to take care to work with more than a single picture.[36] The metaphor of the Body of Christ says a great deal about relationships, mutual responsibility, gifts and unity. However, it says very little about mission, about grace, about the Church in time and in eternity. Other images and models become essential here.[37]

Image and sacrament

At the very centre of the service of Holy Communion, in response to the ministry of the Word and before the ministry of the sacrament, the president reminds the congregation of their identity in the words quoted at the head of this chapter. The words most commonly used, in the form given here, are taken from a number of passages in the New Testament.[38] Again, the central metaphor used, which catches the interrelationship of Christians with one another and with Christ in Scripture and in the tradition, is the picture of the Church as the Body of Christ. The language is intentionally linked and powerfully developed in the New Testament and in Christian liturgy to the great sacrament of the Eucharist. We express our unity as the church, the Body of Christ, by partaking in the bread broken in Communion, the Body of Christ. As we break the bread we remember the body of Christ given for us in Jesus' death on the cross, by which we are reconciled to God and become part of the church, the Body of Christ. There is an overlap and overlay between the physical body of Jesus given over to death, the image of the church as the Body of Christ and the Body of Christ in Holy Communion which enlarges, enriches and expands our understanding.

Imagining the Church of the Future

Picturing the church of the future cannot simply be a case of borrowing ideas which work from elsewhere or attempting to keep things going as they are by new forms of ministry. The New Testament and the whole Christian tradition place a significant and high priority on relationships within the Church, the Body of Christ. A church which conceived of belonging through attendance at Sunday worship and occasional voluntary commitments would never have adopted as the prime metaphor for these relationships the image of parts of a body. We are called to form genuine communities. As we fulfil that calling, we need to take care to avoid the dangers of fragmentation, insularity, and rigid adherence to a programme which expects all small groups to behave in a similar way. The transforming communities' model offers one template for such a way forward.

The kind of Christian community envisaged by Matthew is one in which relationships are deep and real enough to demand the regular forgiveness which is essential in close families. This, in turn, implies a way of building Christian community which allows and enables relationships to grow to that point.

Is this true in your experience of the church?

What does it mean to be a member of the Body of Christ?

How can the local church be enabled to have a vision for the wider Church?

Are we called to form genuine communities? If so, how is this best expressed?

9

A Light to the Nations: The Church in Relation to God's World

'You are the light of the world. A city built on a hill cannot be hidden. No one after lighting a lamp puts it under the bushel basket, but on the lampstand, and it gives light to all in the house. In the same way, let your light shine before others, so that they may see your good works and glorify your Father in heaven.'[1]

The Christian church is called into being by God's love and God's grace. We are called to offer to God our worship and praise in our prayers and songs but also in our lives. God calls us not only into a relationship with the Father, Son and Holy Spirit but also into a close relationship with one another: we become, quite literally, members of one another, part of one Body. Our relationship with God and our relationship with one another needs to find its expression in our patterns of belonging and association within the church: hence the need in many churches for more deliberate and intentional small communities for the purpose of prayer, for making real this notion of being part of one another and for Christian formation and growth.

However, we do not yet have a complete picture. A rounded view of the church must contain a third perspective: how are we called to relate to God's world of which we form part and in which we live?

And how is this relating to be worked out in practice not only in our individual lives but in the lives of our churches and our small communities?

The Light of the World

One of the images which threads through the whole of the Scripture is the image of light. The creation of light is one of God's first acts in bringing the world into being. At the end of the Bible, we read that there is no darkness at all in the new creation 'for the Lord God will be their light'.[2] A favourite description used in the Book of Isaiah for the servant of God who will come is that of a light to the nations: 'I am the Lord, I have called you in righteousness, I have taken you by the hand and kept you; I have given you as a covenant to the people, a light to the nations, to open the eyes that are blind, to bring out the prisoners from the dungeon, from the prison those that sit in darkness.'[3] The servant takes upon himself the destiny and the mission of the people of God. The fulfilment of the prophecy in Christ is celebrated in the Songs of Zechariah and of Simeon:

> 'By the tender mercy of our God,
> the dawn from on high shall break upon us,
> to give light to those who sit in darkness
> and in the shadow of death,
> to guide our feet into the way of peace.'[4]

> 'a light for revelation to the Gentiles
> and for the glory to your people Israel.'[5]

The image of Jesus as light in relation to the world is, of course, picked up very powerfully in the Johannine writings.[6] In the quotation from the Sermon on the Mount given above, in 1 Peter, in references to light and darkness throughout the Epistles and in the seven lampstands in the Book of Revelation, this image of the bearer of light is used, by extension, of the church of Jesus Christ. The church is called to reflect, to carry, to bear witness to the light of Christ in every generation to the world around.

However, Jesus' words in the Sermon on the Mount are a reminder to us that the church in every generation, including the first disciples, has been all too ready to relegate this aspect of its common life to a secondary place. Matthew 5:14–15 is both a remarkable statement of faith and a solemn warning. It is a remarkable statement of faith because it is a reminder that the Christian minority in every generation are able to make a huge difference to the society around them by bearing witness to the light of Christ. It is a solemn warning because the church in Matthew's day and ours is in perpetual danger of attempting to hide its light under the bushel basket. We become so preoccupied with being the people of God that the church withdraws into itself and no longer gives light to the wider society.

It is impossible therefore to understand, describe or develop an understanding of the Christian church which does not embrace the concept of God's light and love reaching out to the whole of the creation at least in part through the witness of Christian people individually and acting through the church. We must not, however, fall into the opposite error of supposing that the God of the whole of creation gives light exclusively through the Christian church. The church herself is, as yet, all too imperfect. The witness we give to God's love is incomplete. The Father of creation, we believe, is working in many different ways throughout the universe. Jesus is the light of the world, not simply of the Christian community. The Spirit still broods wherever there is darkness and chaos, striving to bring about a new creation. The disciples go out from Jesus and find that God is already at work in surprising ways which they know nothing about. In the same way our sharing in the mission of God to the world will be a delightful discovery that God is already at work in many situations, individuals and communities who do not yet own the name of Jesus – sometimes in ways which put the church herself to shame. The church is called to bear witness to the light and to be a light in this world which God loves, but in such a way that we are able humbly to recognise God's grace at work through other people, groups and agencies.

The Mission of the First Disciples

As we explore the ways in which the church is called to express God's love for the world, again we turn to the Gospel accounts of the first community of disciples, focusing in this chapter on the great story of Christian mission told by the evangelist Luke. One of Luke's great themes is the Holy Spirit's empowering of the church for mission. The story of Jesus' own ministry begins with his baptism by John at the River Jordan when 'the Holy Spirit descended upon him in bodily form like a dove.'[7] The first act of Jesus' mission is to preach in the synagogue at Nazareth and to lay claim both to this anointing of the Spirit and the mission given to the Messiah by God:

'The Spirit of the Lord is upon me,
because he has anointed me
to bring good news to the poor.
He has sent me to proclaim release to the captives
and recovery of sight to the blind,
to let the oppressed go free . . .'[8]

Note that this first expression of the mission of Jesus in Luke is not a simple evangelistic message of repentance and faith in Christ. It is a message which embraces the whole of society: poverty, captivity, blindness and oppression are to be confronted. This is the mission in which the disciples are called to share and to which the church must give her life. Within that mission, for certain, we must set the task of calling men and women to a new relationship with God in Christ and to membership of the new community, the church, but without losing sight of this broader picture. The call of the first disciples, in Luke, emphasises this task of winning individuals within the wider scope of God's mission to the whole of creation: 'from now on', says Jesus to Simon, 'you will be catching people.'[9]

One of the features of the Gospel of Luke is the way the call of the disciples to mission oscillates between what we might describe as the wider mission of the kingdom of God (to proclaim justice, relief from oppression and wholeness) and that part of mission which is calling individuals to Christ and gathering the new community. Partly for this purpose, no doubt, Luke describes not one but two occasions when Jesus sends out his followers. In the first instance, the mission of the twelve, the emphasis is on Jesus entrusting to the disciples the whole mission of the kingdom: 'Then Jesus called the twelve together and gave them power and authority over all demons and to cure diseases, and he sent them out to proclaim the kingdom of God and to heal.'[10] The later and more far-reaching mission of the seventy-two is similar but different. This time the disciples are sent out in pairs, to every town where Jesus intends to go. They are still to proclaim the whole message of the kingdom but the emphasis here is much more upon gathering a community, following the metaphor of the harvest: 'The harvest is plentiful, but the labourers are few; therefore ask the Lord of the harvest to send out labourers into his harvest.'[11]

The Two Ways

Throughout its history, the church has often become confused about these two different but closely connected ways of relating to the world. On the one hand, the wider mission of the kingdom is about the whole way in which society is formed and structured as well as about the relief of poverty, sickness, need and oppression within that society. Sharing in God's mission is thus an outworking of the commandment to love our neighbour as ourselves and to be a good steward of the whole of creation. At an individual level, it means each Christian discovering our vocation to love and serve God's world, to the best of our gifts and ability. Mission seen in this wider sense of proclaiming the kingdom embraces seeking justice for the poor, working for peace and reconciliation throughout the world, and appropriate care for the environment God has entrusted to us. Engaging in God's mission will often mean the church and individual Christians working in and through partnership with many other individuals, groups and agencies who may not share our allegiance to Christ but who share our desire to pursue the values of the kingdom of God (and who may have much to teach us about that process).[12]

On the other hand, undoubtedly part of Christian mission in the New Testament and throughout church history is the task of proclaiming to others the message of the love of God revealed in the ministry, death and resurrection of Jesus and calling individuals to follow Christ as members of the new community, the Church. This is the activity which is expressed so well in the phrase 'catching people'; this is the harvest referred to in the instructions to the seventy; this is the activity referred to in the Great Commission at the end of the Gospel of Matthew:

'All authority in heaven and earth has been given to me. Go therefore and make disciples of all nations, baptizing them in the name of the Father and of the Son and of the Holy Spirit, and teaching them to obey everything that I have commanded you. And remember, I am with you always, to the end of the age.'[13]

Whenever the church reduces its way of relating to the world simply to the task of making disciples, something hugely important is lost. We are left with the picture of the church as the Ark of Salvation: all we are called to do is draw people into it to safety from the destruction around them. In this picture, 'the world' is no longer a manifestation of the wisdom and love of the good creator but a hostile environment from which we ourselves must escape, within which we must keep ourselves safe and from which we will eventually be taken into heaven. However, when the church focuses upon proclaiming the kingdom of God in all its aspects except that of calling people into a new relationship with Christ, again the message is woefully incomplete. To know the length and breadth and height and depth of the love of Christ is the fulfilment of what it means to be human. The Christian gospel is, as Paul writes, the power of God for the salvation, transformation and healing of all those who believe. Without the faithful proclamation of the gospel and the making of disciples, the new community of the church cannot be renewed in every generation. Evangelism is only part, but an essential part, of the wider task of God's mission in which the church is called to share.

We are all conditioned and shaped by the Christian communities in which we first learned the gospel and our churches today continue to perpetuate a tradition of mission which emphasises one of these elements at the expense of another. So in the same town, it is possible (and, indeed, normal) to find neighbouring churches of the same denomination who go about this task of relating to God's world in very different ways. In one, St Agatha's, there is a formative and strong tradition of God's goodness in creation and God's Spirit and grace at work in the whole of human society. This is combined with practical care for those on the edge of the society. The church works in partnership with the local social services, churches, other faith communities and charitable groups to serve the neighbourhood. Its meagre human and financial resources are freely directed towards providing lunch clubs for the elderly, facilities for parent and toddler groups, groups for English language teaching, victim support groups and benefits advocacy. The congregation are growing older, however, and there are only a few, now, able and active enough to share in resourcing this activity. It would be very difficult to find out more about the Christian faith in an accessible way for anyone who came new to St Agatha's.

St Bertha's down the road is a different story, however. The community at St Bertha's has been shaped by a very different tradition: one which emphasises God's work in redeeming individuals through Christ's death on the cross. The task of the church is therefore very simple: to reach out to non-believers and to build up Christians for this task of witness to the world. St Bertha's common life is therefore entirely focused on communicating Christian faith and building up discipleship within the congregation. Its worship is lively and attractive. There is a range of groups and courses for different age groups and stages of discipleship, including an excellent course for enquirers which is offered regularly. St Bertha's tends to work alone rather than putting energy into partnerships with other groups or agencies. If you visit the church on Sundays, you will find a large, lively and thriving congregation of all ages. You may look in vain, however, for evidence of a concern for justice, for the poor, for God at work beyond the boundaries of the congregation, for a wider desire to love your neighbour as yourself.

Those who identify with one or other of these traditions will, I hope, forgive the element of caricature in these portraits. In one sense at least St Agatha's and St Bertha's have something of a sense of mission and an awareness that they are called to reach out beyond their own boundaries. There are hundreds of churches throughout the land, I suspect, which have no self-conscious sense of mission at all and are simply dedicated to keeping things going for the congregation as best they can. But as the church stands at the beginning of a new millennium and as we look back to the roots of our tradition in order to reshape our common life, we are simply falling short of what the church is called to be unless we are able to embrace God's mission in its fullness: service within the whole of society and the call to make disciples.

Mission and Transforming Communities

How does this understanding of the way in which the church is called to relate to the world affect the lives of small communities within the life of a congregation? The first point to make is, surely, to emphasise that if we see these small communities as at all important as a manifestation of the life of the church, then they must embrace a dynamic of mission. As it has become clear, to see the church as called by God introduces into the life of these small communities a foundation of grace, of being accepted by God and therefore accepted by one another. The response to the overflowing grace of God is the offering of our lives, expressed in the life of the small community by commitment to one another and by praise and worship as the core of our common life. Secondly, to see the church as formed into the Body of Christ through God's grace is to put a new priority on relationships within the Body. We need to come to know one another well enough to learn from one another, to support one another in our discipleship, to assist one another in discerning gifts and calling. In this way, Christian community enables Christian formation and growth in discipleship. Thirdly, to see the church as a light to the world and called to demonstrate and tell of God's love for the world must also mean that if small communities are to be genuine expressions of the Body of Christ, they must themselves have some outward dynamic and focus.

The discovery of gifts and vocation

First and foremost, this sense of mission will need to be expressed through the energy and life of the group being invested in taking time to support one another in discovering each person's gift and vocation for service in the kingdom of God and in living out that vocation. We are each called to live out our discipleship not only in a church-based context but in our families, network of friends, work, leisure activities and wider community. These contexts need to be brought into the life of the group (as well as into public worship) through story-telling, sharing of joys and difficulties, space for prayer about key personal decisions, and honesty about challenging areas of Christian discipleship. A group whose agenda is set entirely by worship, Bible study and intercessory prayer is unlikely to have space for this kind of activity. The way in which individuals who form its life are supported in their daily lives through meeting together will be, as it were, incidental to the main agenda: the real business of the group may well happen over coffee at the end of the evening. If time can be given to this aspect of life however, as relationships grow and develop, so does the community's capacity for support. The teacher may be able to reflect with the group about how to deal with a particularly disruptive pupil in a Christian way and to pray with her small community about the problems a disruptive child is creating; someone starting up a new business will be able to offer the project to God; someone who is out of work will be able to communicate something of the helplessness created; someone who is reflecting on a call to become a Reader may test out how the group would respond.

Reflecting on a changing culture

The second way in which transforming communities might enable those who are part of them to live well for God in a complex and changing world is by providing an opportunity and context for reflection and discussion about a changing society. How Christians relate to the culture around them has always been the subject of debate: different perspectives are found within the Scriptures and at every stage of Christian history. The more rapid the sense of cultural change, the more pressing the need for Christian people to have the opportunity to think about the culture they inhabit and how they should respond. What should I make of my teenage children's engaging with the virtual community of the Internet? How should we begin to read the latest manifestation of fantasy literature? How do Christian people adjust to the changing patterns of Sunday, of leisure time and of their working life? How am I to use the active years following early retirement? Why do older and younger people seem to be inhabiting such different worlds? How are the roles of men and women changing in our wider society? Christians in most generations have needed to confront a certain amount of cultural change (but have not always negotiated that change successfully). The church in the twenty-first century will probably face more significant cultural changes and upheaval than any previous generation. We will not respond well simply to being told how to react to this change. However, we are likely to welcome an opportunity to engage with the issues with others who are concerned about them. This too is about learning to live in and engage with God's world.[14]

Discovering a vocation together

In the story at the beginning of the book, an important milestone in the life of the first transforming community was taking on a particular project together – in this case the support of a parent and toddler group which met in the local church hall. In some ways, this can seem something of an artificial exercise. In another, however, thinking through a project together is not only useful in itself (in that energy and prayer are invested in something which is good for its own sake) but the project is indicative that the group is meeting not simply to satisfy the needs of its members but also to reflect and be a sign of God's kingdom in the wider world. Exploring the kind of project a transforming community might invest time in can itself be an exploration of what Christian mission can include. The projects might be in the church, the community or the town; they might be local, national or overseas. This kind of enquiry enables a group to discover more about the gifts of its members than an exercise which is focused solely on ministry within the Christian community. A group is enabled to learn about individual vocation and gifts by thinking through what kind of project it might be right to take on together. The project itself will no doubt yield many important lessons about collaboration, perseverance, celebration and difficulty. Almost certainly, the project will involve learning about an aspect of community, society or the world which will be new to certain group members.

Hopefully, all of the groups at some point or another will want to include in their expression of Christian mission some attempt to build community and communicate faith among their own circle of family and friends. In practice, some groups will do this naturally without, as it were, trying. These are usually (and not surprisingly) groups which have among their members people who are gifted in different ways as evangelists. Others may find it harder. To make a set rule that all groups are to engage in the process of sharing faith at all times and therefore should expect to grow in number (as in some forms of cell church) seems to me not to be a liberating and life-giving guideline. However, some kind of hope that, in appropriate ways, the small groups will participate in the mission of the church to make disciples is entirely realistic and appropriate. If the whole church is operating on a process model of evangelism then it is relatively easy to see how a small initiative mounted by a single small group might fit into the overall picture of sharing faith.[15] As indicated in the last chapter, the group itself will in any case be a vital part of the local church fulfilling the command to make disciples: this is the place where formation and transformation are taking place.

Supporting the wider mission of the Church

Although the small community expresses a vital part of what it means to be church, it cannot express the whole either in terms of worship, fellowship or mission. As described in Chapter Five, there are many aspects of Christian mission which cannot be adequately expressed by a handful of Christians meeting together. In our present context in British society, the Christian Church has many opportunities to act as an institution both in relation to care for individuals and their families (through the pastoral offices) and in relation to other institutions (such as schools, hospitals, prisons). Some of these relationships will be expressed at the level of a single parish or congregation (as when the minister or lay representatives are elected to a school governing body or a parish takes on a long-term project such as work with the homeless in a particular district). Some of these relationships will be expressed at the level of a larger group of churches such as a circuit or deanery (as when ordained and lay representatives are consulted and involved as part of a local authority or regional redevelopment scheme). Other regional opportunities may come through a diocese or Methodist District. Still others will come to the churches at national level and are vital, appropriate and legitimate expressions of Christian mission, with the potential to affect the lives of thousands of people for the better.

One of the slight dangers of a congregation or small group discovering its own vocation to mission is that today's re-emphasis becomes tomorrow's overemphasis, drawing in all available energy and resources. The lives of transforming communities need to find a level such that they are genuinely supporting the Christian lives and vocation of those who form them and are undertaking worthwhile projects for the sake of the gospel, yet those who are part of such groups have, over a period of time, the energy and the freedom to become involved with and give time to these larger, institutional projects.

The Church as Sacrament

In each chapter of Part Three, we have taken a moment to reflect on the links between our understanding of the church and our understanding of the sacraments, especially the sacrament of the Eucharist. God calls the church in grace: Holy Communion is the sign and sacrament of that grace: God's provision for the people he has called together. God calls the church in grace to be the Body of Christ. In the Eucharist, we celebrate that through the death of Christ we are united not only with God but with one another: 'We break this bread to share in the body of Christ. Though we are many, we are one body, because we all share in one bread.'[16]

As we think of the church in relation to God's world, it is immediately clear that both the sacrament of baptism and that of the Eucharist are mission shaped and centred. Baptism is the outward sign of new birth in Christ: of membership of the new community. The Eucharist is the meal by which God's people are drawn together, renewed, nourished and transformed by both the Word of God and through Christ's presence in bread and wine and sent out again to share in God's mission to the world.

In a deeper sense still, however, theologians in ancient and modern times have portrayed the Church as a sign of God's particular presence in and through the world. This theme of seeing the Church herself as a sacrament has been a theme of Roman Catholic theology since the middle of the twentieth century.[17] Again the link is made with the image of the Body of Christ. If we are indeed to describe the Church in this way, then clearly we are called to reflect Christ's presence not simply to one another but in the wider world.

The Power
of the Holy Spirit

As mentioned above, Luke pays particular attention to the Holy Spirit's empowering of the ministry of Jesus. In the same way, in Acts, Luke describes for us in some detail the link between the gift of the Spirit on the day of Pentecost and the empowering of the church to share in the mission of God to the society in which it was set:

> When the day of Pentecost had come, they were all together in one place. And suddenly from heaven there came a sound like the rush of a violent wind, and it filled the entire house where they were sitting. Dividing tongues, as of fire, appeared among them, and a tongue rested on each of them. All of them were filled with the Holy Spirit and began to speak in other languages, as the Spirit gave them ability.[18]

Luke builds upon and draws from a number of Old Testament passages here which speak of the empowering of the Spirit of God, particularly Ezekiel's vision of the valley of the dry bones.[19] The army of dry bones can only live when God's breath or spirit, symbolised by the wind, comes into the bones and grants life. So, according to Acts, the church is only enabled to participate in the mission of God to the world when empowered by the same Spirit of God. The gift of the Spirit at Pentecost is not described by Luke as a once and for all experience. At each major junction in the story (and at other points as well) we are reminded of the importance of the gift of the Spirit in taking forward God's life and love into the world.[20] In the same way, in our congregations and small communities, we will need to pray for the empowering gift of the Spirit to enable us to share in God's mission in our individual calling, in the tasks we undertake as small groups, and in the Churches' wider institutional work within society.[21] We are called to build small communities of God's grace, affirming and accepting people as God has called them, bound together into one Body in which each feels the joy and pain of the other and empowered by God's Spirit for mission and service in God's world.

Is your church more like St Agatha's or St Bertha's?

What questions is our culture asking members of your group just now? How can you facilitate reflection on those questions?

Look again at the five marks of mission (above p. 89f.). Give examples of how each of these might be worked out in a transforming community.

How does the Holy Spirit empower the church for mission today?

10

Pilgrims in Progress: The Church in Relation to Time

> Every foreign land is to them as their native country and every land of their birth as a land of strangers.[1]

We have surveyed the origins of the church in the beginning and in every generation. The church comes into being through the call and grace of God. We are called to the praise of God's glory and to reflect the life and fellowship of Father, Son and Holy Spirit in our common life. We have examined the kind of relationships into which we are called within the church as members of one Body, building one another up in maturity and discipleship, to the measure of the stature of the fullness of Christ. We thought in the last chapter about the church in relation to God's world: our calling is to be salt and light – to extend God's love to the whole of society and to the whole of creation and to participate in the mission of God in the world in ways appropriate to our gifts and calling.

However, our portrait of the church is not yet complete, even in outline form, until we have grasped something of its story and standing in relationship to time. We have seen the beginning of the story in God's calling of the people of Israel, in Jesus' gathering and sending of the disciples and in the stories and writings of the early Church. But we have not yet seen how the story will end. The church is far more than a human organisation, set up by a group of founders many generations ago and perpetuating certain habits and a way of relating internally and externally. There is more to the story, even, than seeing the church as sustained and guided through the presence of the risen Christ and the power of the Holy Spirit. To understand the way the church is and is called to be in the present, we must also understand something of the end. Throughout the Scriptures, the New Testament writers appeal to the destiny and future of the church as a way of explaining the present and as a means of encouraging the young communities. The most important part of the story is, in some ways, still to come.[2]

The Christian Hope

It is no exaggeration to say that the whole of the Christian faith looks forward. As we have seen, the prophets of the Old Testament foretell the coming of God's kingdom and God's Messiah. Jesus comes proclaiming that 'the kingdom of God has come near'.[3] The understanding which emerges as the consensus in the New Testament is that Jesus established the kingdom through his ministry, death and resurrection: a new era has begun. However, we do not yet see a complete fulfilment of what is foretold in Scripture. The whole Church and the whole of creation is waiting in hope, straining forward to the day when the reign of God is complete. For this reason, Jesus teaches his disciples to pray, 'Your kingdom come. Your will be done, on earth as it is in heaven.'[4]

According to all of the four Gospels, Jesus teaches his disciples through parables, images and in clear and direct language that in some way beyond our understanding and at some point in time known only to God, he will return. This theme is a major one in a series of parables which run through the Gospel of Matthew (some of which are also recorded by Mark and Luke). Many of them refer directly or indirectly to the life of communities of disciples in the time before the final appearing of the king and the last judgement. So, for example, the parable of the weeds among the wheat addresses the problem that the Christian community is such a mixed group of those who bear fruit and those who do not. It will not always be so. There will be a time when both wheat and weeds are harvested: one will be harvested and the other destroyed.[5] In the story of the labourers in the vineyard there is a time of labour and then a time of reckoning at the end of the day.[6] In the parable of the ten bridesmaids Jesus gives clear instructions to the church to keep

149

awake, to watch and be ready for the return of the bridegroom.[7] In the parable of the talents, the master first entrusts his property to the slaves, then goes on a long journey until, after a long absence, he returns for the final reckoning and judgement.[8] Other passages in the Gospels describe the coming of the Christ and the last judgement in much more direct language.[9] The disciples are commanded to be watchful and to live each day in the light of the Lord's return: 'Keep awake therefore for you do not know on what day your Lord is coming.'[10] New Testament scholars have studied the sayings about the return of Jesus very carefully. It seems clear that the earliest documents in the New Testament originate in communities which anticipated that Jesus would return within the lifetime of the first disciples. Little attention, therefore, is given to the establishing and ordering of the church as a long-term Christian presence in the world. In later documents, however, we see a different under-standing developing. Luke, in particular, sees a new era beginning with the ascension of Jesus and the gift of the Spirit at Pentecost. This is to be the era of the Church and it will endure until Christ himself returns:

> So when they had come together, they asked him: 'Lord, is this the time when you will restore the kingdom to Israel?' He replied, 'It is not for you to know the times or periods that the Father has set by his own authority. But you will receive power when the Holy Spirit has come upon you; and you will be my witnesses in Jerusalem, in all Judea and Samaria, and to the ends of the earth.' When he had said this and they were watch-ing, he was lifted up, and a cloud took him out of their sight. While he was going, as they were gazing up towards heaven, suddenly two men in white robes stood by them. They said, 'Men of Galilee, why do you stand looking up toward heaven? This Jesus, who has been taken up from you into heaven, will come in the same way as you saw him go into heaven.'[11]

The Church therefore lives in the time of 'now and not yet'. The kingdom has been established but not yet fulfilled. For individual Christians, the journey ends with death and resurrection to eternal life. For the Church as a whole, however, the task of 'keeping watch' continues until the Lord returns. The fulfilment of the kingdom embraces not only the community of the Church but the whole of creation. Paul draws out in Romans 8 the blessing and the challenge of living in the perspective of 'now and not yet' both for the creation and for the Christian community:

> I consider that the sufferings of this present time are not worth comparing with the glory about to be revealed to us. For the creation waits with eager longing for the revealing of the children of God … We know that the whole creation has been groaning in labour pains until now; and not only the creation, but we ourselves, who have the first fruits of the Spirit, groan inwardly while we wait for adoption, the redemption of our bodies. For in hope we were saved. Now hope that is seen is not hope. For who hopes for what is seen? But if we hope for what we do not see, we wait for it with patience.[12]

In much simpler language, Paul writes elsewhere: 'For now we see in a mirror, dimly, but then we will see face to face. Now I know only in part: then I will know fully, even as I have been fully known.'[13]

The eternal destiny of both creation and the church is a major theme of the Book of Revelation. The end point for both is something so different from the mixture of hope and frustration we encounter today that it needs to be described in the radical language of a new making: 'Then I saw a new heaven and a new earth: for the first heaven and the first earth had passed away, and the sea was no more. And I saw the holy city, the new Jerusalem, coming down out of heaven from God, prepared as a bride adorned for her husband'.[14] The picture given of the church in Revelation is, according to Kevin Giles, 'both a statement of faith about what the church is in God's sight now and a declaration of how it will be seen by all in the near future'.[15] The eternal reality and the end point of history are identical.

Pilgrims, Aliens and Strangers

This concept of the church not being 'at home' in the world as it is because we are travelling to something better, something which is promised but has not yet been given, underlies a final group of images or pictures of the Church in Scripture: that of pilgrims, aliens and strangers. The picture of a pilgrim people lies beneath the description which was the first name by which the Christians were known: followers of 'The Way'.[16] This metaphor in turn draws upon three other powerful biblical images. The first is the language developed in the Old Testament about the Way of the Lord.[17] The second is that of the exodus from Egypt. The people of Israel have been set free from slavery. They are travelling to the Promised Land but have not yet arrived there. God sustains them with food for the journey. They travel in community, being shaped by the experience into the people God calls them to be. In several of the New Testament writings, parallels are drawn between the journey of the Exodus and the experience of the church, which has also been set free from slavery and is travelling to the Promised Land.[18]

The final picture evoked by the language of the Way is that of Jesus travelling with the disciples: the journey is to be one of faith, made in the company of others, travelling the way of the cross. The pilgrim image of the church and of the Christian journey has been taken up in different ways in the Christian tradition, most powerfully in John Bunyan's allegory of the journey of an individual Christian. The tradition of groups of Christians making a pilgrimage together as a journey of formation and discovery about faith goes back to the time of the New Testament and remains a much valued tradition to this day.

The picture of aliens and strangers emphasises not so much a journey towards a new future as the experience of living in the world yet not being quite at home here. The image is not as prominent in the New Testament as that of pilgrim: it is an important theme in 1 Peter,[19] as we have seen, and in Hebrews[20] and there is some reference to the concept in Ephesians.[21] At its root is not the experience of the people of God in the exodus from Egypt but the experience of the Jews in exile from their homeland with the implication that they will one day return. This experience shaped much of the Old Testament and is therefore a strong theme in the Epistles. As applied to the Christians, the new meaning given is that the Christians scattered throughout the world are one community in many lands. They are not waiting for the day when they will return to the land of Israel but looking forward to the time when the whole Church is called home and reunited in the new creation. Although the language of aliens and strangers is not used in the fourth Gospel, the great prayer of Jesus in John 17 contains very similar concepts of the Christians being in the world yet united with Christ. The image of aliens and strangers is one which becomes important in the first centuries of the Church, not least in the Epistle to Diognetus quoted at the head of the chapter:

> For Christians are distinguished from other men neither by country, nor language, nor the customs which they observe. For they neither inhabit cities of their own, nor employ a particular form of speech, nor lead a life which is marked out by any singularity ... They dwell in their own countries but simply as sojourners. As citizens, they share in all things with others, and yet endure all things as if foreigners. Every foreign land is to them as their native country and every land of their birth as a land of strangers ...
>
> To sum up all in one word – what the soul is in the body, that are Christians in the world. The soul is dispersed through all the members of the body and Christians are scattered through all the cities of the world. The soul dwells in the body, yet is not of the body, and the Christians dwell in the world yet are not of the world.[22]

Now and Not Yet

What does it mean for the church to live in this now and not yet time? What does it mean to be united with Christ and with the saints in heaven yet to live as aliens and exiles in the world – to be always not at home here and longing for something else? What does it mean to be a pilgrim people travelling towards a different future? Four related aspects of the church's life in the now and not yet time need to be considered. Each is important for our expectations in shaping the life of the church today.

Imperfections

One simple, if entirely obvious, implication is that the church shares in the imperfection of creation and the imperfection of the world. This is true in the most general sense and the most particular and local. The Church throughout the world is imperfect, flawed and mistaken. The Church as we see her throughout history has made terrible errors of judgement, has given in to numerous temptations,

153

has drifted off course regularly and on numerous occasions. Whatever denomination we belong to, it ought to be possible to be aware of inherent weaknesses and besetting temptations and struggles. At the level of the local church, the picture will be exactly the same. Any congregation will, hopefully, get some things right but will also make many mistakes and wrong turnings. The church is not a community of perfected saints but a gathering of pilgrims in progress. There is a Christian T-shirt slogan which reads: 'Be patient – God isn't finished with me yet!' A sign with similar words might be hung in every church doorway and called to mind at every planning meeting. The great Reformers expressed the same truth more elegantly in their Latin watchword *ecclesia reformata et semper reformanda* which translates (less elegantly) as 'the church has been reformed and always needs to be being reformed'.

In the parable of the wheat and weeds, and elsewhere in the Gospel of Matthew, Jesus addresses this mystery of how we are to respond to the reality that the church is such a mixed community of those who are seeking to be true disciples and those who do not produce good fruit in their discipleship. The problem recurs throughout the New Testament. The answer in the parable is that, generally speaking, we are to do very little. There may be exceptional occasions when it is appropriate and right, in a considered way, for the church to exercise discipline over its members, particularly where scandal is created in the wider community. For the most part, however, attempts to 'purify' the church and to create the true Christian community within the larger whole are impossible. Worse still, in attempting to pull up the weeds, the growth of the wheat itself will be disturbed. Creating an atmosphere of judgement instead of grace within the Christian community will damage the church more than the imperfections of its members.

This message needs to be heard and understood by any church which attempts to develop small communities for worship, fellowship, formation and mission. Often such initiatives are seen by those who begin them (or by those who resist them) as an attempt to draw together the 'true' church within the wider Christian community. If only we can gather together those who are truly committed to following Christ, we will make real progress in the Christian life. The message is 'heard' that those outside such groups are therefore not 'proper' Christians and a dynamic of mutual judgement grows in place of the dynamic of grace. Over time, however, it becomes clear that those who have formed the new, smaller community, are actually quite a mixed bunch as well. There are those who seem to take their discipleship seriously and those who seem to be attracted by the coffee, or the attention they will receive, or the possibility of influencing others. And so the whole process may need to begin again. If only we can gather the true believers together ...

In practice, of course, any group of Christians will be imperfect. Any group will contain people with a whole mixture of motives for being there. Any group will contain those who are growing in their faith at this particular time; those who are drifting away; those who are in particular need. A church which establishes transforming communities needs to be aware that, whilst there are many, many good reasons for moving in this direction, the strategy will not lead to a perfect church, nor will those who gather together in such groups necessarily be those who are the 'better' Christians. We are on the Way but we will not arrive in this lifetime.

Frustration

In the story of the first man and the first woman in the garden, one of the consequences of disobedience is that the ground itself is cursed and brings forth food only after much toil, sweat and difficulty.[23] As I read the stories in Acts and the letters of the New Testament I receive a similar picture of what Christian ministry and life in the church is to be like. There are certainly moments of great progress and fruitfulness: the great healing miracles (which are miracles precisely because they do not represent what is normative in the life of the church); the growth of the church after Pentecost; the mission to Ephesus. Overall, the big picture is one of the confident and steady expansion of the Christian faith in the ancient world in a remarkable way. But as we look more closely, we also see that this progress is uneven. For every three steps forward there were often two steps back. After every great victory there are defeats and setbacks. Where churches are established and flourish, as we can see from Paul's letters, there are also many problems which arise and need to be overcome. There is wonderful fruit for the gospel, but in the midst of great labour, toil and difficulty.

As we look around the Church today, wherever in the world we might look, it is a similar picture in reality, although the picture can

155

be distorted by sensationalised accounts of growth on the one hand or doomsday scenarios of unmitigated decline on the other. Christian ministry is both very hard and very fruitful. Again this means that in approaching the possibility of establishing transforming communities (or any other initiative in the life of the church) we should not be deceived into imagining that any such way forward will be a cure for every ill or some magic formula which will guarantee instant and trouble free 'success'. Moving forward in the life of the church will always involve a high degree of toil and sweat: like growing vegetables in a garden where the soil is not good and the ground is full of weeds.

Suffering and struggle

'I consider that the sufferings of this present time are not worth comparing with the glory about to be revealed to us', writes Paul in Romans, contrasting the present time of the pilgrimage with the future rest and hope.[24] The story of the Exodus is more a story of suffering and struggle, as a model for our pilgrimage, than it is a story of comfort and ease. In Psalm 23 the shepherd leads the sheep through places of great darkness and trouble as well as still waters and green pastures. In *Pilgrim's Progress* Christian's adventure leads to him encountering a number of different troubles, trials and temptations, most of which contain some elements of difficulty. The experience of going on pilgrimage today is very often one of a journey which is, in some way, difficult. Part of the growth which comes through pilgrimage is a result of facing those difficulties in the company of others.

Again, we should be under no illusions that suffering and difficulty will characterise the life of Christians and the life of the church. Christians are not immune from the normal troubles which strike every person in this life: the consequences of ageing and breakdown of health; accidents and unexpected illness; work and relationship difficulties; bereavement and death. There are other difficulties which may arise more specifically from being a Christian and maintaining a positive and attractive Christian witness in a hostile environment: in family, school or workplace. To be members of one another as the Body of Christ means to be open to the suffering of others rather than avoiding it. In so far as a church is a living Christian community, therefore, it will almost always be experiencing suffering and struggle to some degree and will need the resources of Christian endurance, love, faith and hope to see that suffering transfigured and changed to glory.

As Christians share their lives to a greater degree and casual acquaintances become friends, brothers and sisters, this common experience of suffering will become a greater and deeper reality. In resourcing transforming communities, therefore, churches will need to bear in mind the need to teach more, not less, on such subjects. The cost of commitment and community will need to be explored and understood by all who take part.

This will not be an easy road yet it is a good one. My favourite illustration in the Good News Bible accompanies Galatians 6:2: 'Help carry one another's burdens and in this way you will obey the law of Christ.' The picture is of a line of people travelling together in the same direction, each with his or her own burden, but all helping one another. This is one aspect of what it means to be church. It also illustrates part of what it means to be a transforming community.

Conflict

In its journey, the church experiences difficulties in itself, difficulties in the terrain it must travel through and difficulties arising from the normal experiences of life. The Scriptures bear witness to a fourth kind of difficulty on the pilgrimage: that of conflict which arises not simply from constant and continual difficulties within oneself or the general environment, but difficulties which seem to arise from what might best be called 'strategic opposition' to Christian growth, progress and formation. The early Christians (and the Church throughout the centuries) used the imagery of a spiritual battle:

> For our struggle is not against enemies of blood and flesh, but
> against the rulers, against the authorities, against the cosmic
> powers of this present darkness, against the spiritual forces of
> evil in the heavenly places. Therefore take up the whole armour
> of God so that you may be able to withstand on that evil day
> and having done everything to stand firm.[25]

The image is taken up in the service of baptism where the minister
makes the sign of the cross on the forehead of each candidate and
says: 'Do not be ashamed to confess the faith of Christ crucified'. The
congregation then say to the candidates:

> Fight valiantly as a disciple of Christ,
> against sin, the world and the devil,
> and remain faithful to Christ to the end of your life.[26]

Again, the witness of the saints down the ages and of Christians
today is that many worthwhile endeavours and new ventures in
Christian mission and ministry prove to be unreasonably difficult:
things go wrong at key moments and in ways we do not expect.
There remains a sense of conflict, difficulty and opposition to
progress in the kingdom of God. Those who seek to establish small
missionary communities should expect to meet it.

The heavenly banquet

Each chapter in Part Three has attempted to establish links between
our theological understanding of the church and our understanding
of the sacraments. Again, this is important when looking at the
church's understanding of the future hope. Baptism is the sign and
seal of new birth in Christ, the sacrament of initiation into the
Christian community which consists both of the Church on earth
and of the communion of saints. The Eucharist expresses the truths
explored in this chapter in two ways. Firstly, the image of food for
the journey, drawing on the gift of manna in the wilderness and
Christ as the Bread of life, is a pilgrimage picture. We travel often
through harsh and difficult terrain in which the people of God need
to be sustained by God's grace. Secondly, the Eucharist looks not
only backwards to the Passover, the Last Supper and the death and
resurrection of Christ but forwards to the fulfilment and realisation
of the kingdom of God. Our worship is joined to the worship of

heaven and we look forward together to the great heavenly banquet:

> Send the Holy Spirit on your people and gather into one in your kingdom all who share this one bread and one cup so that we in the company of all the saints may praise and glorify you for ever, through Jesus Christ our Lord.[27]

> May we and all who share this food offer ourselves to live for you and be welcomed at your feast in heaven where all creation worships you, Father, Son and Holy Spirit.[28]

> Gather your people from the ends of the earth to feast with all your saints at the table in your kingdom, where the new creation is brought to perfection in Jesus Christ our Lord.[29]

Pilgrimage and Transforming Communities

The Archbishop of York, in a recent sermon, finds in the images of pilgrims, aliens and strangers 'a clear emphasis on temporariness and transition, on movement and progression and travelling light – a much needed contrast and counterpoint to the Church as a static and fixed institution'.[30] At the very least, the concept of a pilgrim people underscores the need for the Church continually to reflect on its structures and to engage in a process of change. In my view transforming communities have the capacity to provide exactly these light, flexible structures of worship, formation, fellowship and mission in a variety of ways within local congregations.

However, the image also applies itself well to how a network of small groups might operate in terms of its overall structure and framework. It seems appropriate to see the concept of pilgrimage operating at several different levels. All Christians are engaged in a journey of faith and will be helped in their journey by being part of a transforming community: helped to grow in faith and understanding, to live as disciples of Jesus Christ, and to discover their own gifts and vocation. Each parish church or congregation is also on a journey. Developing a network of these small missionary communities may prove to be an appropriate step on that journey of enabling worship, mission and discipleship in many congregations. However, because each parish church is itself different, the way in which these structures work out in practice in every situation may well be distinct and particular. Thirdly, at an intermediate level, in a church with half a dozen transforming communities, each of them will have its own journey. There may well be some discernible similarities between one group and another and there will certainly be some common problems and difficulties. Equally, there will also be very proper differences in terms of a trajectory of growth and development, agenda, spirituality and vocation to mission. Within each small community, the Spirit of God is at work among the people of God. Each small community will need help and guidance to enable discernment of what is appropriate and right. This guidance will need to be given within a framework which is enabling rather than seeking to standardise and control the small communities' journey of faith.

A Vision
for the Church

In Part Two of *Transforming Communities* we looked at the need for change in the life of the Church in order to respond to changes both in society and within the church. Like Samuel, this generation of Christian ministers is called to transitional leadership: to maintain the present structures of church life but to develop within and alongside them new and creative ways of being church. As a vital part of that process, we need both to understand the process of gaining new vision and to develop that vision. A new picture of the future will emerge from a careful appreciation of the present situation, on the one hand, and a re-examination of our understanding of what the church is called to be and to become on the other.

In Part Three, we have looked at these theological roots of our understanding of the church. We have reminded ourselves (or discovered for the first time) that the Church must not see itself only as a human society but as called out and called together by the grace of God in Christ. God sustains, empowers and guides the Church through the Holy Spirit's presence. Christians are called into a deep and meaningful relationship with one another, as well as individually with God. This relationship is itself transformative of our lives and character and is a vital part of discipleship. It is a relationship which needs to be enabled and resourced by the structures of local church life. The Church is called to share in God's mission to the whole of society. The foundation of that mission is enabling each Christian to live out their discipleship in our wider society. The Church is looking forward to a new future and a new creation: what we see now is incomplete, imperfect; what we experience now is often frustration and difficulty. The suffering of this present time is not worth comparing to the glory about to be revealed in us. The shape of the Church we imagine for the future must be tested against our theological understanding of what it means to be the people of God. I believe that the concept of transforming communities is entirely consistent with and flows from the central ideas of a church called by God, members of one another, a light to the nations and pilgrims in progress. Part Four of the book now looks at practical resources for helping the vision to become more of a reality.

Does the picture of aliens and exiles ring true for the church in our generation? In what ways are we not at home here?

Think through together the evidence which you have seen of:
- imperfections
- frustration
- suffering and struggle
- conflict.

Are these real experiences for the church today?

Look together at the Good News Bible illustration. Is this a good picture of a transforming community? How else would you draw it?

Where do you go from here on the journey?

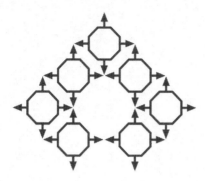

PART FOUR

Enabling
Transforming
Communities

Introduction

It is one thing to develop a clear vision of where you want to go. It is another to begin the journey. There is a limit to what can be said here about the practical side of enabling transforming communities. On the one hand it would be wrong to attempt to be over-prescriptive: if the vision outlined here is at all near its target as a way of re-imagining the church then there will be many different ways of bringing it about. Every context is different but God is the same. We need to rely as much upon the Spirit as upon the wisdom of others. On the other hand, developing transforming communities as a primary way of developing the life of the local church is, in itself, a practical task for which most of us need some guidance both to make a beginning and to keep things on course. These two final chapters of the book attempt to strike a balance therefore between offering too little practical advice such that you have no idea where to begin and too much so that you become bogged down in the detail and begin to think the directions for the journey are more important than the destination.

The chapters are structured in such a way that I hope you will be able to use them as the basis of one or more practical training sessions both for a small steering group attempting to develop transforming communities in the parish and for those called to be leaders of transforming communities. I've tried to direct you to other resource material which might be useful here as well.

At the beginning of Part Four, it may be as well to remember the vocation to transitional leadership which was the conclusion of Chapter Two. The particular calling of this generation of lay and ordained church leaders is to a church in transition. We are called both to sustain the life of the church as it is and to see change and transformation from within for the future. The central part of the book has attempted to give content to that new vision and direction. As we come to the practical outworking of this vision, we need to keep in focus again the dual nature of this calling.

11

Planning
and
Policies

1. Beginning the Journey

The material in this chapter and the next consists largely of practical ideas for moving forward in the general direction outlined in *Transforming Communities*: towards building up within the life of the local church these small, enabling, missionary groups. For some readers of this book, the ideas contained here may be obvious and not really needed: you already have a blueprint in your mind or come to the task with a great deal of experience of forming this kind of group. However, others of you may be very conscious that forming, guiding and sustaining communities of this kind is not a straightforward task: wisdom, energy, grace and insight are needed. This is true if you are beginning from a low base and nothing similar exists at the moment. However, it may also be the case if you inherit a situation in which a church is part-way there. Changing an existing network of homegroups into the kind of communities envisaged here may be more complicated than it seems.

It is impossible to put all of the practical help needed into a book and even more impossible to draw it out again for a wide variety of different situations. This chapter looks at some of the areas of planning and policy any church needs to address before beginning to establish transforming communities. Chapter Twelve examines issues connected with sustaining the communities once they have begun and about developing the groups as the building blocks of local church life. At the end of each section of this chapter you will find a short summary box, usually in the form of a question. These questions have been designed as a guide for your local ministry team or steering group. You probably won't be able to work through them all in a single session. There is enough material in this chapter for three or four meetings of a planning group.

Every local church, therefore, which begins to go down this road will benefit from an external advisor who can act as consultant or midwife to the process: discerning with those responsible where you have come to and where you might be going. Bringing about change in a context which we ourselves are part of is a difficult business. More often than not, we need the encouragement, wisdom and support of someone else who is outside the situation. Remember that the kind of changes in church and community life which are envisaged here do not take place in an instant: a period of several years is needed before the culture of any institution can begin to change. Remember also that the work in which you are engaged belongs to God and is accomplished as much by prayer as by forming policy and taking action together. Move forward in confidence that God has supplied and will supply the gifts and resources which are needed. Keep the picture of a journey in your minds: it is not necessary to map out the whole route before you make a beginning. Often the lessons of the first part of the journey are essential to discern the direction when you come to the next crossroads. New possibilities and horizons open up which cannot be anticipated at the starting line. We are changed ourselves as we move on together.

Before you begin:

Have you taken stock of where you are now?

How will you find and develop a relationship with an external consultant?

How will you commit this journey to God in prayer?

---

2. Ownership and Decision-making

A major shift in the policy of a local church to develop transforming communities should not be made either lightly or because it is the bright idea of one or two individuals. Before any moves forward are made, therefore, it is important to engage with three preliminary questions.

Teaching about the nature of the church

A key part of renewing vision in the life of the local church is, as we have seen, nurturing the picture of what the church is and is called to be by God. It is likely that the starting point for this new departure in the life of the congregation will be some fresh teaching around this theme. The resources in Part Two may be of some help here, together with other materials provided by a diocese or denomination.[1] The material might be delivered through sermons, one or more study days, a residential or non-residential parish weekend, through a pattern of existing groups, a special Lent course, articles in a parish magazine, or a mixture of all of these. The teaching should be in such a form that there is the opportunity both for input (and especially biblical study) and feedback and discussion. Ideally, this focusing of the church's teaching . programme should be advertised as a preliminary to new developments in the life of the parish. You will, no doubt, have some resources within the life of the congregation to take this forward. However, this is also a key point at which to draw in others to help. The exercise may be one you have to take forward as a single congregation. Ideally, you might want to work on the ideas as a group of parishes in a locality, deanery or circuit. Even better, invite a range of congregations from different churches in the area to come together for this.

Discernment of vision

Once this part of the process is under way, it is important that the work of renewing the whole vision of the local church is put in hand, following a process similar to that outlined in Chapter Three. This will involve, no doubt, a small co-ordinating group with different people tasked to undertake the basic map-making and audit of both the congregation and the local area. The group will need to work at understanding the history of the church and the community. This process will need to be established and owned by the principal decision-making body in the church, with the support of the ordained minister(s), and whatever small group undertakes the work will doubtless report back to this group with a number of recommendations. Ideally this reporting back process will involve as many as possible in the whole congregation, with some provision for the action group to test out their ideas, refine them and bring them back for final approval. Time will be needed both in the small action group and the wider meeting to listen to God as well as to undertake this work together, so that an attempt is made to discern the right direction for this particular congregation at this particular time. At the point at which the group reports back, the pathway of your particular church may begin to diverge from the pathway of forming transforming communities which is outlined here. Your discernment might be that a different way forward is the right one for you. Your discernment might be that you are called to merge with a different congregation in the same area or that the most important priority is to undertake a large building project. Many visions are possible. However, these chapters are written in the belief that establishing transforming communities may be an important step forwards for many churches in the United Kingdom at the present time.

Appointment of a steering group

The decision to develop new communities should not be taken by one or two individuals. The steps needed to establish new communities should not be directed simply by a few individuals either. The story at the beginning of the book is told, in this respect, much too simply in outline, implying that all energy and initiative comes from the person who is ordained. In practice, that person would need behind him or her a group of colleagues who are praying together, reflecting on progress and sharing their common life. As the ministry documents of the Diocese of Durham state clearly, the sharing of Christian ministry only comes about through the sharing of lives.

Therefore, once a church or group of churches has decided to embark upon this journey it will need to establish some kind of steering group if there is no existing structure already in place. Many churches, of course, already have local ministry teams or other structures of collaborative leadership.[2] Where these already exist, the decision-making bodies simply need to entrust this group with taking the vision and policy forward. Where they do not, it is essential that such collaborative structures begin to develop alongside the vision for transforming communities.

However, it is vital that any such Local Ministry Team or steering group should be more than a committee or decision-making body. A group which is designed to oversee the building of community must itself take great care that it becomes a community, sharing at least some of the characteristics of the network of small groups it hopes to nurture and see flourish in the life of the local church. This means that the steering group itself will need to give time at its meetings to the sharing of stories and of vision, and to worship and study together, and will need to grow through at least some of the different stages which are outlined below. The members therefore need a similar commitment to that called for in members of transforming communities: to learn and grow together; to share their lives to some degree; to pray for and support one another in this journey.

Once a congregation has passed through these stages of teaching about church, of discovering and discerning vision and of establishing a Local Ministry Team or steering group, it is ready for the next stages of the journey.

Ownership and Decision-making

How will you enable the whole congregation to reflect on the nature of the church?

How have you engaged (or how will you engage) in the process of developing new vision for the church in your locality?

Do you need to develop a Local Ministry Team or steering group?

---

3. Making Connections

As we noted above, sociologists have begun to use the term 'social capital' as a way of giving value to the many different kinds of relationships which together contribute to an overall sense of community, which in turn makes an enormous difference to the ability or inability of our broader society to work for the well-being of its members.[3] In essence the framework for developing the church outlined here is about refocusing a sense of Christian identity and of Christian mission through the intentional development of missionary community and therefore of social capital. The best and most effective way to bring this about in many situations will be through the forming of new groups for this purpose. However, this deliberate new initiative (which may not be possible everywhere) should be set against the backdrop of a general shift in emphasis in the life of the church to create relationships and community: to generate growing social capital. In many congregations this will be a necessary preliminary step to the forming of new transforming communities. We are very unlikely to commit to meeting regularly with a small group of people unless we have at least some idea of what they may be like.

How can we begin to increase and develop any church's stock of social capital? When the congregation meets for public worship, a shift in this direction is possible through the creation of attractive space and time for interaction before and after (if not during) the service. Congregations need to understand that this is part of being church. The value and potential of these times can be greatly developed through thoughtful investment in what is made available. Is the space such that people are able to mix with one another? Is there somewhere to sit down comfortably so that more substantive conversation is encouraged? Is there an area where children can play quietly, mix with their own friends and not disrupt the conversation of the adults too much? Are the refreshments of sufficient quality to communicate that this is a worthwhile and important exercise? Is there a gentle 'hosting' of the event either formally or informally such that newcomers are not left standing on their own and people who do not know one another can be introduced and encouraged to form links? Other elements in public worship will encourage the building of community. Is the style of preaching such that the congregation are able to form a relationship with those who preach and lead worship? The provision of the right kind of information for the intercessions can help or hinder the building of community. Occasional interviews with different members of the church within worship as well as being helpful in themselves can serve the wider end of helping people get to know one another.

Outside of Sunday services, the church stock of social capital is increased whenever people meet together with the focus on building relationships rather than undertaking a task. Encouraging hospitality is an obvious route. A vital part of the Christian tradition from the time of Jesus onwards is the sharing of meals together in one another's homes. There are few better ways for getting to know an individual or a family. Again this can be encouraged and facilitated in different ways through the work of a shared ministry team. For any church to begin to move away from the pastoral model described in Chapter Four (see p. 50f.), those responsible for ministry need simply to concentrate their efforts on building the links and relationships between different members of the Body of Christ so each is less dependent upon the relationship formed with the pastor. The formal development of small groups simply builds on and builds up this informal network of relationships which can be encouraged and facilitated within a Christian congregation.

Throughout this informal process, care should be taken to ensure that the building of community links takes place not simply between members of the same church but between members of the church and the wider community. Putnam describes two different kinds of social capital: *bonding* between members of homogenous groups and *bridging* which forms a network of links outside those groups within our wider society.[4] One of the most disturbing conclusions of his book is his analysis of religious participation where he concludes that:

> the community-building efforts of the newer denominations have been directed inward rather than outward thus limiting their otherwise salutary effects on America's social capital. In short, as the twenty-first century opens, Americans are going to church less often than we did three or four decades ago and the churches we go to are less engaged in the wider community.[5]

Churches, like other institutions in our society, influence the patterns of lifestyle and behaviour in ways that are life-changing and transformative. In most cultures in our society they can play a role in demonstrating and encouraging patterns of hospitality. However, if these patterns of hospitality relate only to bonding with other members of the church then the kind of community that is established will be difficult soil in which to grow genuine transforming communities. The kind of group that will grow most naturally in such ground is one that has fellowship rather than mission as its focus. If a pattern of hospitality can be encouraged which is genuinely open and seeking both to build up Christian fellowship and continually build bridges with those beyond the church then the soil is being prepared for the planting of small groups which will genuinely be open and prepared to reach out in different forms of mission. In the words of Jesus:

> 'When you give a luncheon or dinner, do not invite your friends, your brothers or relatives, or your rich neighbours; if you do, they may invite you back and so you will be repaid. But when you give a banquet, invite the poor, the crippled, the lame, the blind, and you will be blessed.'[6]

Making Connections

How will you develop the relationships between members of the congregation:

- in or around Sunday worship
- through midweek events
- through encouraging and enabling hospitality
- in a way which bridges as well as bonds?

---

4. Overcoming Objections

The most common objection I have encountered in over ten years of teaching some of this material in embryo form to groups of clergy and lay leaders is that some churches are simply not open to the possibility of an ongoing network of small groups. There are a number of different reasons for this – some of which may apply in one situation and some in another.

- It may be an issue of commitment (in that people simply are not taking their discipleship seriously enough to offer more than occasional attendance on Sundays). This problem is likely to affect many other areas of church life and any attempt to move forward in any direction. It needs to be tackled directly and grace-fully through prayer, preaching, teaching and care.
- It may be an issue of time: people's lives are far too busy to give up an evening a fortnight to this kind of community. This is genuinely the case in some contexts – particularly for those in mid-life – but will only rarely be true for the majority of a congregation. Appropriate ways of steadily building community need to be found as a substitute for ongoing groups. These can include occasional courses, days or weekends away. Inevitably, building relationships with others always does entail some investment of time. Where the lack of time is caused by an over-busy church life this also needs to be addressed (see the next section).
- It may be an issue of culture: people's established notions of Christian life, faith and church regard anything like transforming communities as odd, extreme, eccentric – something for a certain kind of Christian. If this is the case, establishing a new network of small groups is likely to be very hard work – but that doesn't mean it isn't worthwhile or the right way forward. Headway will almost certainly be made with at least some people through preaching, teaching and conversation. The opportunity to visit or hear from churches which are part way down this road can be useful. In the end, it will probably be necessary to begin with a small group of those who are willing to try the idea and let the concept grow from there. Those who become Christians as adults as part of a small nurture group are often willing to go on meeting.

- It may be an issue of trust: individuals or the general congregation may be afraid to commit themselves to other people in this on-going way because they have been let down in the past. This may also apply to the minister(s) or others sharing in leadership in the church. Where trust has broken down then it needs to be rebuilt, primarily through establishing relationships and building a network of community.

Overcoming Objections

What objections are you likely to encounter to this way forward?

What do you think lies at the root of them?

How will you seek to overcome these objections in order to move ahead?

---

5. Simplicity and Subtraction

When my family moved to the house where we now live in September 1996 there was a small tree in the middle of our back garden. Our four children, who went to climb the tree, found a large number of very small apples growing all over it. They were much too small to be of any use and I concluded that the children had discovered nothing more than a crab-apple tree. But I know next to nothing about gardening. A week or so later my father came to visit and went to look at the 'crab apples'. In fact, he told us, the tree was a normal apple tree that had simply not been pruned by the pre-vious owner of the house for some time. Instead of bearing good fruit, therefore, it could bear only these tiny sour apples. Dad pruned it for us very drastically. The following year next to nothing happened. But the year after and every year since we have had a good crop of cooking apples from this tree we thought was simply decorative.

Many (if not all) local churches tend to run at slightly more than their capacity in terms of the energy of their ministers and active members. There is often so much going on that what fruit there might be is choked and does not reach maturity because there is no space for it to grow. The reasons for this overcrowding and lack of pruning are many and various. Projects are easier to begin than to close down in the life of the local church. None of us like conflict. We can often be motivated by the needs of others and so begin initiatives without the proper resources to see them through. If a church is declining in the full-time ministry available to it or the numbers of active members, it is likely that the remaining resources will be stretched to capacity. There may simply be no energy therefore to begin any new project. The pruning knife needs to be taken to the tree before good things will grow again. Space needs to be created, with love and care. We need to practise subtraction before we can do addition. We need to do less, well in order to achieve more.

How and where can this subtraction be done? There is no blueprint. It will certainly be something which needs to be considered by a shared ministry team or steering group rather than an individual. A key concern in the early stages of the process will be to create time and space for reflection and development in the lives of those who will be most active in pioneering transforming communities. This will normally mean the stipendiary minister, the shared ministry team and any others who may be closely involved. Good new developments will not be possible if this group of key people are continually working at full stretch to sustain what is there already.[7]

Almost certainly, if a church is moving from over dependence upon the clergy to a more self-sustaining model, there will need to be a double learning of the habits of letting go. The people of God will need to let go of dependence upon the stipendiary clergy (in such matters as administration, maintenance of the church building and, very often, instant availability in moments when some kind of pastoral care is needed). The clergy in their turn will have to let go of their need to be needed in these kinds of crises and, occasionally, of the habits of living always at full-stretch and from crisis to crisis. The church may want to consider cutting by half the amount of time it gives to administrative meetings (simply by meeting every other month instead of every month, for example). Organisations and groups which really do depend upon the presence of this key group in order to happen will need to be looked at most carefully. Should they be preserved or allowed to die? The whole church will need to own the necessity to create some space so that new growth is possible. A significant element in the art of transitional leadership will be the discernment of when it is appropriate to sustain a meeting, a service or an organisation and when it is appropriate to allow such a venture to be closed or to die. Only rarely should such a decision be made on the grounds of avoiding conflict and division. Hard choices are normally necessary in most worthwhile endeavours.

The basic direction of the pruning, however, should be apparent from the previous section. If the ministry team is seeking to create a fruitful and healthy environment for the development of transforming communities, then they will want to preserve especially those elements of church life which foster and build relationships among members of the church and with the community outside and let go of elements which do not serve this end to the same degree. The Mothers' Union meeting over tea and cake which binds together a group of older women in the parish may be a vital part of this interconnectedness (although the vicar may not need to be present for this to happen). The midweek service to which only five people come who then go straight home again may be less important.

At a later stage in this development, once transforming communities begin to meet regularly, then space will need to be created by subtraction not only for the steering group or ministry team but for the whole congregation. At this point in the process, it will be necessary for much of the life of the church to be progressively devolved from the central structures of the congregation to these small groups. A church will find it impossible to sustain, for example, a programme of whole church social events and a network of small groups who meet regularly for fellowship with others. A traditional missionary committee may find that its events are much less well supported because each transforming community is giving priority to its own mission project. Old ways of relating and doing church will give way to new. The task of the ministry team will be to oversee this process allowing some projects to give way to others as the life of the church is transformed from within. It is likely that both ministers and ministry team will particularly need the help and support of external consultants in discerning where and how subtraction can begin.

Simplicity and Subtraction

How can the working pattern of the stipendiary ministers be pruned and simplified to give space and time for (a) reflection and (b) the development of transforming communities?

Ask the same question for the Local Ministry Team or steering group.

What do you think you need to let go of in the life of your local church in order to enable new patterns of life and mission to grow?

---

6. Policies and Guidelines

There are basically two alternatives for a church in establishing trans-forming communities from scratch. The first is to begin with a single group as a prototype and then apply the lessons learned as new groups are begun from this original community. The new groups are formed by those who have been part of the original group. The second is to establish a number of new communities at the same time. This second route is likely to be more demanding on those whose task it is to prepare and sustain both the leaders and the groups. However, the balancing factor is that more people are able to be involved in the process more rapidly, giving a sense of the whole church moving forward together. How you will proceed at this point is a key question for the Local Ministry Team or steering group.

In establishing a single group which will lead to a network or attempting to establish a new network of groups it will be vital that the church reaches a common understanding of what such groups might be like, how often they could be expected to meet and what they will do together. Some kind of agreed statement which catches all of this will be important as part of simple publicity for the groups and as a way of inducting new groups and new members once they are established. It might well incorporate some kind of expression of commitment which the members make to one another as well as general expectations articulated by the whole church. One example of such a statement is given in the panel overleaf:

Transforming Communities at St Bartholomew's

As part of our vision for the future, St Bartholomew's is seeking to establish a network of small missionary communities of Christians who meet together, seek to build one another up and support each other in their Christian life and engage together in God's mission to our world.

We hope that this will lead to the whole church growing together in faith, love, discipleship and Christian mission.

These small communities are open to all members of the congregation and to those who are outside the church.

We anticipate that each transforming community will consist of between six and ten members who agree to meet together once a week in the initial period when the group is being formed and thereafter twice a month. Meetings will normally be in the homes of group members. The groups will be enabled by two convenors, appointed by the Church Council and publicly commissioned at the Sunday Eucharist.

The meetings themselves will include opportunities to get to know one another; prayer together; some study and reflection; support for one another in the whole of our lives and, after the initial period, undertaking Christian service and mission together.

The transforming communities will be linked to Sunday worship in a number of ways including, at certain times of the year, common study material designed to help the groups reflect upon the preaching.

The members of the group undertake to:

- be committed to group meetings
- support one another in prayer and in practical ways
- undertake some form of Christian service together
- grow together as a building block in the life of the church.

We hope that some, at least, of the transforming communities will grow in numbers as well as in the quality of their common life. Groups will therefore need to be open to the possibility of giving birth to new communities as the numbers involved increase over the coming years.

In order to draw up a statement like this, a Local Ministry Team or steering group will need to work through their answers to a number of questions.

What will you call the groups? Some generic title is helpful. 'Transforming communities' may not be the best one. Some churches also have a tradition of individual groups choosing a name for themselves as part of establishing an identity.

Will you have an open policy? In my view, this is by far the best way forward. The group itself needs to be free to recruit and draw in new members both from within the congregation and, sometimes, outside it. These may be people who are on their way to faith or those who are part of other churches in the area who do not offer such a network of small communities. A system of small groups where all members need to be referred by the vicar or some other central person can be very restricting.

What is the ideal size of group? Beginning with six to eight people is about right in most circumstances. This size of group can be accommodated within most homes, which solves the problem of where to meet. More importantly, it is small enough to mean each member is important and able to make a contribution. In the early stages, getting to know individual members is a manageable task for the group convenors. Once a group reaches twelve or so members it is normally appropriate to begin to think of birthing a new community.

How often will the group meet? This needs to be determined as much by social context and people's availability as by anything else. In some areas, those who are church members may have a great deal of time available for ministry and mission outside their work and home life. In many other areas, this time will be strictly limited and therefore need to be very carefully thought through. Any group will grow together far more quickly if it can meet together each week for the first six to eight weeks of its life. Thereafter, many groups are able to sustain a common life by meeting twice a month but also giving time to shared mission of various kinds. It is, of course, very possible to imagine trans-forming communities within the same church which meet with different frequencies: those which meet, say, once a month for a longer time, or those who sustain their sense of community through virtual meetings as well as face to face.

How will the convenors be appointed? Again, some policy is needed, together with some kind of job description and outline of the support which is offered. Examples are given below. The title you give to the convenors needs to be defined. It is important that there is some shared sense that this ministry is authorised by appropriate authorities within the church and that there is public recognition, celebration and prayer of this vocation to sustain small missionary communities. The number of convenors in each group needs to be at least two in order to facilitate a collaborative model of ministry, to provide a conversation partner for reflection and to provide space for developing new leaders for the new groups which may be needed. The support and sustaining of these convenors is dealt with below.

How will the life of the groups be linked to Sunday worship? Again, there are a number of different possibilities. If there are no formal links, then it is possible that the Sunday and midweek life of the congregation may pull apart. If there are too many links, this will tend to exclude rather than encourage those who are part of the church on Sundays but unable or unwilling to take part in the small communities. Some pattern whereby the sermons are linked with the life of the groups at certain points in the year is likely to be helpful.[8]

How will new groups be formed? In an initial start-up period it is possible to develop new groups either by beginning with a single transforming community drawing others in and this group giving birth to new communities or attempting to begin several groups at the same time. After that start-up period there are again two possibilities of seeing the number of groups grow through existing groups becoming larger and establishing new groups from these (which is dealt with in the following chapter). However, it is also possible to establish new groups through drawing enquirers and those on the edge of the church together to explore the basics of the Christian faith, through Alpha or an Emmaus nurture course, and giving that group the opportunity to continue as an embryo transforming community. In this way a church might see the number of these communities grow by one or two each year as described in Chapter Five.

Policies and Guidelines

Draft a statement of intent for the congregation.

Drawing up the statement will mean answering the following questions as part of your planning:

What will you call the groups?
Will you have an open policy for membership?
What is the ideal size for a group in your context?
How often will the groups meet?
How will leaders or convenors be appointed?
How will you link the groups with Sunday worship?
How will new groups be formed?

---

7. Developing and Sustaining Leaders

One of the keys to developing small communities in the life of the church will be the development of those who might act as convenors or leaders of these communities and enable their common life. In some situations, there may be a ready-made pool of people who have the necessary gifts, skills and experience. In others, substantial prayer and training may be needed before the appropriate people are ready to take on this responsibility. The number of groups in a church can only increase at the same rate as suitable leaders are developed. A certain amount of advance preparation of such leaders is essential. It is important that those who will facilitate the groups have a shared understanding of the vision. It is particularly important that those who have been formed by previous experience of small groups in church life have the opportunity to see and understand that the transforming communities vision is different in at least some important ways. Material for such advanced preparation can be found in this book. A number of other agencies have developed leaders guides for small groups, some of which are referred to in the next chapter.

Advanced preparation is one thing – ongoing support is another. The latter is an area where churches often fall short. Projects begin with enthusiasm but are not followed through because lay leaders lack the necessary means of support and oversight in their task.

Both the classic Cell Church and the Metachurch models of small groups have recognised the need for very high quality and frequent coaching support for the leaders of small groups within an extensive church network. They also recognise that, within any church with more than four such groups, this proactive support and coaching cannot be provided by the stipendiary minister. Both groups recommend, therefore, the development of an intermediate ministry of proactive coaching and support for group leaders. Ralph Neighbour calls these ministers 'Zone Servants'.[9] In the Metachurch system of Carl George, the group leader who facilitates a community of ten is called a cell group leader and designated by the Roman numeral X (ten). The intermediate minister is called a coach and signified by the Roman number L (fifty).[10] The biblical precedent for both systems is the story of Moses and Jethro discussed in Chapter Four.

The addition of this intermediate ministry, even in comparatively small networks of groups, gives very significant structural strength to an emerging network. With the introduction of zone servants or coaches, there is the capacity for continuous reflection on the life of each small community, for continued training for the group leaders and the energising and development of the whole network. Without them, if the support of group leaders is simply another task of the stipendiary ministers, the whole network is in danger of simply keeping going or slipping into decline. Transforming communities are not the kind of plants which can be placed in the soil and left to grow come rain or shine. Like vines, they need the right trellis and continuous care in terms of tying up, pruning and weeding until they bear fruit.

A stipendiary minister (S) seeking to manage a group of emerging transforming communities without this intermediate ministry would soon be in a similar position to the vicar of a pastoral church described in Chapter Two:

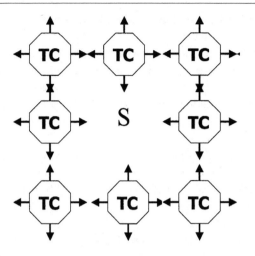

Figure 9.

It's not easy to see how the numbers of transforming communities can continue to grow. The structure is therefore somewhat self-limiting. However, if the intermediate ministry of leader coach is developed, with each leader coach sustaining five groups, the over-all structure is greatly strengthened and a pattern is developing which can be multiplied and still remain strong:

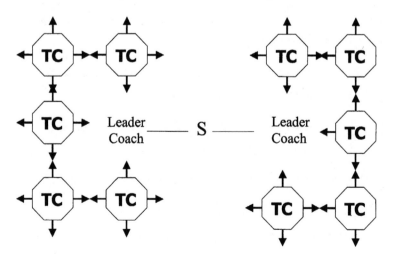

Figure 10.

185

Three other clusters of five transforming communities can be added to this structure before it is anything like 'full'. At that point, the minister will be relating proactively to five leader coaches, the leader coaches to five group leaders, and the group leaders to 8 to12 group members. All of the ministers could well be non-stipendiary. Space has been created for up to 250 people to be sustained in discipleship, mutual care, ministry and mission in a manageable and extendable way.

Carl George also identifies an excellent and workable model for meetings of what he describes as the leadership community (the minister or ministry team, the leader coaches and the group leaders) built around the acronym VHS: Vision – Huddle – Skill. For the first forty minutes of each meeting, the whole leadership community is together for worship, prayer and sharing in common vision. For the second forty minutes the group of leaders 'huddle' with the leader coaches sharing common concerns and providing mutual support. For the final third of the meeting the focus is on building the skills of the leaders in some way through workshop based training. The leader coaches also visit the groups in their care from time to time and offer proactive support and guidance to the leaders. George's approach is jargon-rich and may for that reason be off-putting to some. However, he has developed proven principles for sustaining an extensive network of small groups and small group leaders in a way which does not exhaust the energies of any individual and still leaves room for continuous growth.

Developing and Sustaining Leaders

How will leaders be identified, appointed and commissioned in their ministry?

Will you develop the intermediate ministry of leader or group coaches?

How will the leadership community meet together?

12

Forming a Transforming Community

The focus of the practical help in this chapter[1] is the week by week life of a transforming community from its foundation to maturity as a group and the support which will be needed by its leaders or convenors. The advice given assumes that the congregation have engaged to some degree with the ideas in the book as a whole: that there is widespread ownership of this way forward by the congregation and by those responsible for its life, some basic policies have been defined and a reasonably clear understanding of what establishing transforming communities as basic building blocks of the church will mean.

For the group leaders, drawing together a group of eight or so individuals and seeing them formed into a missionary community is itself a demanding and complex task and one which is often underestimated. In terms of the meetings themselves, the group will move through a number of different stages.[2] Throughout the whole period of a group's life, the leaders need to be aware of the educational and community process taking place in its life at two levels and the way in which they fit together. The *macro process* is that of the group's life over a period of months and years. The *micro process* is what takes place within a given meeting. The way in which the micro-process is adjusted and developed affects the macro process of the group.[3] A typical trajectory might be something like Table 3 (allowing for some flexibility of interpretation, particularly in matters of timing).

TABLE 3 The Development of Transforming Communities

Stage 1	Stage 2	Stage 3	Stage 4	Stage 5
Early develop-ment	*Later develop-ment*	*Early maturity*	*Maturity*	*Rebirth or ending*
1–3 months	3–9 months	6–18 months	1–5 years	18 months–5 years
Strangers form a community.	Honesty and affirmation. Some conflict.	Task begins: supporting one another and discerning mission project.	Task continues: supporting one another and under-taking a project each year.	Making a good ending and sharing in the birth of new groups.
Focus on story-telling with some worship and study.	Focus on worship and study with some story-telling.	Focus on supporting each other and mission project with some worship, study and story-telling.	Focus on supporting each other and mission project with some worship, study and story-telling.	Focus on celebrating what has happened and planning for the future.

Stage 1: Early Development

1–3 months

A significant aspect of the leaders' ministry in the early stages will be diaconal: about serving the members of the group through finding the best location; providing meals or refreshments; arranging transport; providing clear directions and guidance and the right kind of welcome. As the group grows and develops it will, no doubt, be appropriate that these tasks are shared. However, at the early stages much may need to be done by the appointed group leaders.

In its first weeks together, the priority in forming a new group is simply for people to get to know one another through being enabled to tell their stories of life and faith and begin to share together some of their hopes, dreams and vision for the future and for this new group. This is how relationships grow. At this stage, telling stories of life and faith to one another is not simply a pre-liminary to the main business of the group – it *is* the main business of the group. The most natural sharing and conversation will, of course, happen informally over coffee or meals together, on walks, or as members begin to spend time together outside of the group meetings. Structuring the time the group spends together in a formal meeting, however, can go a long way to facilitate this process. As with most endeavours of this kind, the leaders will need to judge the appropriate level of sharing and this judgement will guide both the kinds of questions which are asked and their own level of self-disclosure. 'Tell the story of when you left home' may be an appropriate first question for the second or third meeting of a new group. 'What is the most difficult thing that has happened to you since you became a Christian' is probably better saved for a later meeting.[4]

Some groups and cultures will take very naturally to this kind of sharing together. Others will need to move towards it slowly and, sometimes, indirectly. Group leaders will find that unless they are able to share at least something of themselves in this way then the group is unlikely to make a great deal of progress in building relationships. Good clear guidelines will also need to be given on confidentiality and on establishing good practice in giving one another space, listening attentively and non-judgementally if community is to grow. The leaders will also need to guide the group as it begins to find the most helpful way for prayer and worship together at this point in its life.

At this early stage of the group's development, the following timetable may be appropriate for a two-hour meeting:

- A simple meal together (30 minutes) or 30 minutes for coffee and cake at the end of an evening.
- Opening prayer, news and brief reminder of the purpose of the group and any ground rules you have established (10 minutes).
- Sharing together based around one or two questions, structured

so as to enable the group to tell each other about different aspects of their stories and lives (30 minutes).

- A short biblical reflection with some questions and answers around themes of Christian community, the nature of the church, or similar themes (20 minutes). Much will depend here on how much material has been covered in the church's preparation for beginning transforming communities.

- Prayer together. The way in which this is structured will depend on the spirituality of the church of which the members are part and the emerging spirituality of the group. It is best to begin with prayer which is simple, inclusive and familiar. A simple liturgy with some prayer said together and space for short intercessions would work well. This can be prepared in advance and printed on a handout and the form can evolve as the group's life takes shape. The prayers should collect together the theme of the evening (20 minutes).

- Refreshments and space at the end of the meeting (10 minutes) – or a cup of coffee at the beginning if you were not able to begin with a simple meal.

Although the leaders will need to facilitate most parts of the meeting in the very first weeks, from the early weeks together some of these tasks can be shared out.

The length of this first period of the group's life will depend upon a number of factors. How well do people know each other to begin with? How quickly does trust grow? Is the group broadly homogenous or does it contain significant differences? Are there six people or twelve? How regular are the members in their attendance? If attendance is irregular then establishing the basics of community can take a very long time. A group which agrees to meet every week for the first 6-8 weeks will become established much faster than one which meets twice a month over 6 months.

The key factor in discerning when the group is moving onto the next stage is the degree of honesty of engagement which is beginning to emerge. As soon as the group show signs of this deeper level of honesty, whether through affirmation or confrontation, you are ready to move onto the next stage.

1. Early Development

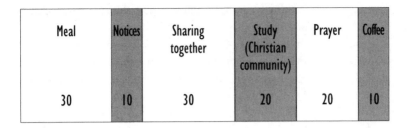

Meal	Notices	Sharing together	Study (Christian community)	Prayer	Coffee
30	10	30	20	20	10

Stage 2: Later Development

3–9 months

A degree of intimacy and trust is needed in any group if its life is to develop to the extent that you are able to support one another in your discipleship and to undertake common tasks. This intimacy and trust cannot develop, however, without the group being able to give and receive affirmation and also to handle conflict and difference. Every analysis and model of teams and groups whether from a Christian or a secular perspective highlights this as important. Many Christian groups do not, however, face conflict and difference particularly well.

Again, the role of the leaders here is particularly important. At this stage it is appropriate for the leaders to be somewhat less directive than in the early phase of the group's development. The aim should be to build a safe space where different members of Christ's Body can be honest with one another about areas of similarity and difference with the overall aim of building up each member of the community.

In terms of what the group does, the emphasis will probably need to move away from sharing together at this point and focus instead on study and learning together. It is easier to learn to express conflict and difference when talking about abstract ideas than events or experiences which may be very personal. A typical timetable for a group in this period of its life may well be something like this:

- Sharing together over a meal. This may be formal or entirely informal depending upon the group. The important thing is that it happens and the group understands that this is an important part of meeting together (30 minutes). An interview or testimony from each member of the group in turn would be an interesting variant on eight people answering the same question.
- Welcome, opening prayer, notices and a reminder of the purpose and vision of the group (10 minutes).
- Study together. This may continue the themes of the first part (the church and the nature of Christian community); or else a study of parts of the New Testament where Christians get to know one another and disagree in the process (for example, parts of the Gospels or Acts or 1 Corinthians). At this point the group may want to use published materials, providing they are adapted to where you are at the present time and led in such a way as to facilitate each person taking part. If the group is made up of quite new Christians, then it may be important to cover some key themes of Christian discipleship through study at this point.[5] If a great deal of study of this kind is needed before moving on to look at mission and outreach then this will clearly extend this stage in the group's life together (45 minutes).
- Prayer together. It should now be possible to begin to build on the pattern of prayer which has been established and on the good relationships which are forming. A time of news and the sharing of requests for prayer will enable the group to support each other in this way. Again, a simple liturgical structure is likely to be very helpful. The group may begin to develop its own simple traditions in prayer and worship such as re-arranging the room or lighting a candle. The prayer should end with some kind of act of dedication by the group to live as Christian disciples in the coming week(s) (20 minutes).
- Space at the end of the meeting for a drink and conversation together (15 minutes).

Most groups, I envisage, would now be meeting fortnightly or twice a month after the initial stage of becoming established. The leaders will be able to discern when a group has moved through this stage as they observe in themselves and in others a growing trust in the group: when disagreement and affirmation can be articulated with courtesy and Christian love and when there is a growing restlessness about task and purpose.

2. Later Development

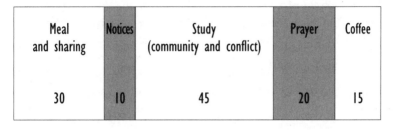

Meal and sharing	Notices	Study (community and conflict)	Prayer	Coffee
30	10	45	20	15

Stage 3: Early Maturity

6–18 months

As the group reaches this point, the leaders will recognise that the basic process of the group forming has happened and will lead the community onto the next stage of focusing on the task of enabling one another in the whole of life and in beginning to discern an appropriate project for mission. From this point onwards, the group is beginning to reach maturity.

The appropriate subject for study in this period of the group's life is, undoubtedly, the nature of Christian mission and the kingdom of God. As this book has argued throughout, this picture of mission needs to be larger than evangelism and sharing our faith although it will include that element. An early focus should be developing the group such that each member is supported in living as a Christian in the whole of their daily life including work, family and voluntary activities.[6] This will mean that a new element is introduced into the sharing: members might take it in turns to describe a particular dilemma or situation which they face. The prayer life of the group will focus more naturally upon intercession. The group may need to look together at questions of Christian vocation, at the nature of the kingdom of God and at mission, as well as at sharing the faith through words.[7]

The value of the group beginning to develop a common mission project is enormous.[8] Energy is released outwards for the building of the kingdom of God. The mission of the church and not simply its ministry is devolved onto the small communities which become transformative not only for their members and the wider church but for the whole of society. Within the life of the congregation, the groups will be seen not simply as places for new or passive Christians but centres of outreach and action. Within the group itself, relationships grow in a different way and new gifts can be developed if the whole group is working towards a common goal. Ideally the mission projects should be far more than tasks undertaken within or on behalf of the church (such as managing the church coffee rota). They should arise out of the study, concerns and Christian life of the group members, giving maximum space for growth, flexibility and the work of the Spirit. The very process of identifying a suitable mission project in the life of the group involves considering questions of need, guidance, resources and vocation as a Christian community which further helps to define and develop the group's life.

During this period of the group's life, the leaders will need to introduce and then develop time in the meetings which is set aside for identifying, beginning and then managing the group's current mission project. This time will need to be greater in the start-up phase than in the ongoing life of the group: indeed at some points the whole meeting may need to be given over to this part of the group's life.

An outline timetable during this period might be:

- Sharing together over a meal. The focus here will sometimes be on a particular member of the group talking about his or her life or work in detail; sometimes on everyone discussing a particular issue; or sometimes general conversation. A group will evolve its own pattern. The leaders will need to remember that the most valuable forms of fellowship are those which do not need to be facilitated intentionally – they simply happen (30 minutes).
- Welcome, opening prayer and worship, notices and a reminder of the purpose and vision of the group (10 minutes).
- Study together. Possible themes for this are described above and include Christian mission; vocation; the kingdom of God; evangelism and life together. The study will need to lead into the

action section of the meeting in some way (25 minutes).

- Taking action together. This section will comprise both discussion of practical outcomes in terms of the discipleship of every member of the group and reflection together on the particular mission project as it is developing. The time will need to be adjusted between study and action as the mission project develops (20 minutes).

- Prayer together. Again, this will build on developing traditions but will focus more, perhaps, on building the kingdom, upon the needs of the world, upon the discipleship and mission of each member of the group and upon the developing mission project (20 minutes).

- Space at the end of the meeting for a drink and conversation together (15 minutes).

An important feature to note about this and other stages is that it should be entirely possible (and, indeed, desirable) for new members to join the group at this or any other point. Wherever possible the leaders and members of a group should be encouraged to draw others in both from the wider congregation and outside it. In this way, the growth of any particular group is organic. The only period when a lot of new people may disrupt the growing community in the group is after the fourth week of the very first stage until the group begins to be established. However, it is very important that group members are inducted properly into the life of the young community through personal introductions and through some telling of the group's story both in the group meetings and outside it.

It may well be that at least some of those who join the group will be on their way to faith or very new Christians. The church as a whole will need to make some kind of flexible policy decision about whether people in this position are to be nurtured and grow in discipleship as part of an ongoing transforming community or whether they should be encouraged to participate in a nurture course which is offered centrally such as Alpha or the Emmaus nurture course. Both have their advantages. Where nurture is offered as part of the group, almost certainly some provision will need to be made for simple teaching, learning and instruction about the very basics of the Christian faith outside of the main group meetings, normally on a one-to-one basis. The group may want to make resources available for this purpose (such as audio tapes, videos or other materials).[9]

Where nurture is offered through a central course then the group is still able to play its part through prayer, friendship and support for the new Christian, sometimes through going with him or her to the first meetings of a nurture course and through playing a part as sponsors in a baptism or confirmation service. In this way the whole church, through its transforming communities, contributes to building the road to faith.

3. Early Maturity

Meal and sharing	Notices	Study (mission)	Taking action together	Prayer	Coffee
30	10	25	20	20	15

Stage 4: Maturity

1–5 years

As the group continues, perhaps over several years, the convenors will need to be alert to ways of continually renewing its life through worship and prayer, and through study and mission together. Different resources will be appropriate at different times, with due note being taken of the wider life of the parish and the network of small groups of which each transforming community is a part.

Again, a parish will need a clear policy on whether the life of all the groups should be linked together through study and through sermons on similar passages or themes. A degree of flexibility and discernment will be appropriate here. At one time it will be appropriate to emphasise diversity and individual community development and at another time unity and being part of the same parish or group of parishes. In most contexts, following standard teaching materials across a network of groups the whole year round would be, I think, to over centralise and lead to stagnation. However, to develop a tradition where the study part of the group meeting is connected to Sunday worship and preaching in certain seasons of the year is very helpful.

Patterns of action will develop on an annual cycle which could helpfully be affirmed by a common Sunday in the year when the mission work of all the transforming communities across a parish was celebrated together. Developing the 'action' side of a group's life will have its own momentum around this annual cycle of adopting projects and seeing them through.

The study side of a group's life will require continual thought and the leaders will need to use their gifts to facilitate the most helpful diet of:

- traditional Bible study following through texts and themes
- thematic study using published material
- issue based study which enables the group to see the whole of society in new ways.

The first two approaches will be more familiar than the third, which has become the classic mode of study from the base communities of Latin America. Instead of beginning with Scripture and using this as a basis for reflection on life, the group is encouraged to begin by seeing the life situation of an individual either within the group or in the wider world and using Scripture as a source for reflection and inspiration for action.[10]

By this point, a group will have developed its own traditions and patterns and need less guidance. The time given to each part of the meeting will also be quite fluid – however the following may be a useful model.

4. Maturity

Meal and sharing	Notices	Study	Taking action together	Prayer	Coffee
30	10	30	15	20	15

Stage 5: Re-birth or Ending

18 months to 5 years

As new members are welcomed in and join the group, the convenors will need to reflect together on whether it is appropriate to work towards the group giving birth to a new community. Once a group grows much larger than a dozen, it becomes quite demanding to lead and a certain degree of intimacy is lost.[11] For developing community, eight is a better starting point than ten. By the time six or eight people have told me their story or answered an ice-breaker question, my attention is beginning to wander.

New communities can be successfully developed from existing groups providing that careful attention is paid to two insights. The first is that care needs to be taken to develop new leaders for the groups. The apprenticeship system developed by the Cell Church movement is a helpful one here. The expectation is that the network of small groups will grow in number. Therefore each group leader aims to have an apprentice who will eventually lead a new group him or herself. The second principle is that a period of adjustment will always follow the establishing of two new groups from an existing larger parent group and each new group must be treated as an individual entity in its own right. In some cases it will be right to go back to basics and establishing community. In others, it may be possible to maintain the original group's place in this journey.

Sometimes it may happen that there is very little numerical growth in the life of a particular group. This does not mean that the group has failed: simply that its charism and vocation is other than evangelism and its own development. It may be possible to sustain the group's life over several years and several mission projects. However, there will probably come a point where numbers and interest begin to dwindle as established members leave or move away (as is common in most churches). At that point, the leaders will need to give thought to whether this community should be brought to an end, taking care to celebrate all that has happened, and energy put into other groups.

Guiding the Journey

It will be clear that guiding and enabling a transforming community through its life and journey is a demanding task. The task of the leader will change and develop as the group evolves, progressing from providing clear direction and good structures at its beginning to enabling its common life in collaboration with the whole community. As much as is possible, the group themselves should approach the development of community and mission together, seeking a way forward through dialogue and prayer. The leaders of the community will also be helped greatly through dialogue and reflection with others in the same church who are also guiding groups and through regular contact and dialogue with a leader coach or someone in a similar role. Shaping the lives of these small communities should not be seen as ensuring that they adhere to a particular programme or timetable. It is much more like the spiritual direction of individuals: the task is to discern what the Spirit is doing in each context and at each stage of the journey and to develop the group in the way that seems most appropriate. Guidance comes in part through suggestion and in part through direction. The different ways in which the group meetings can be shaped will be an important tool, as will the example and discipleship of the leaders themselves. Through the whole process, focus should be on the horizon of the kingdom of God, not simply the horizon of the local church.

Conclusion

Psalm 80 is a fervent prayer for help. The psalm captures a rich sense of God's love and care for his people and combines this with a haunting picture of desolation at their present plight:

> You brought a vine out of Egypt;
>> you drove out the nations and planted it.
> You cleared the ground for it;
>> it took deep root and filled the land.
> The mountains were covered with its shade,
>> the mighty cedars with its branches;
> It sent out its branches to the sea
>> and its shoots to the River.
>
> Why then have you broken down its walls,
>> so that all who pass by may pluck its fruit?
> The boar from the forest ravages it,
>> and all that move in the field feed on it.
> Turn again, O God of hosts,
>> look down from heaven and see;
> Have regard for this vine,
>> the stock that your right hand has planted.[1]

The church in Western Europe has played a remarkable role in the story of Christianity. At the present time, however, that church is in great need of new energy and vision. The problems and difficulties we face cannot be solved simply through the development of a richer understanding of ministry. We need to examine again our understanding of what it means to be church and renew the patterns of community around which we shape the life of the people of God. This will not be the work of a single moment but the task of a generation.

This book has argued that the pattern for this re-shaping needs to be from the local congregation outwards rather than beginning with the denomination, national church or larger unit. Within the local congregation, I have argued, with others, for the recovery of the small missionary community as the basic template for the life of Christian congregations. We have tested this proposal against a theology of the church and against the variety of new directions which are being put forward at the present time as well as exploring the roots of the concept within the Christian tradition. In the hope that some readers of this book at least will want to move forward in this way, there are practical guidelines for how we might begin.

But the place to end is, of course, the place the psalmists begin. Whatever our strategies or structures, they are lifeless without the Spirit. The church, as we have seen, is infinitely precious to God. It is to God alone that we entrust its future and God's power alone which can enable us to move forward in such a way that society around us is blessed and renewed:

Restore us, O God of hosts,
Let your face shine that we might be saved.

Notes

Preface
1. DLT, 1999.
2. *Growing New Christians* (CPAS/Marshall Pickering, 1994); *Making New Disciples* (Marshall Pickering, 1994); *Man to Man, Friendship and Faith* (Scripture Union, 1998); and *Emmaus: the Way of Faith*, eight volumes (NS/CHP, 1996 and 1998) (the latter with Stephen Cottrell, John Finney, Felicity Lawson and Robert Warren).

Part One: A STORY
1. A Story
1. Acts 2:44-7.
2. Acts 13:1–2.
3. Acts 20:28.
4. Acts 2:44–7.
5. Acts 20:32.

Part Two: SEEING CLEARLY: THE CHURCH IN THE PRESENT AND THE FUTURE
2. Moments of Change
1. The Rt Revd Richard Chartres, Bishop of London, in a letter to a newly recommended ordinand.
2. 1 Samuel 7:15–17.
3. Judges 21:25.
4. 1 Samuel 8:5.
5. 1 Samuel 13:19–22.
6. 1 Samuel 8:6–7.
7. The term 'inherited' way of being church is borrowed from Robert Warren, *Building Missionary Congregations* (Church House Publishing, 1995).
8. There are a number of recent studies which chart these changes including Michael Moynagh, *Changing World, Changing Church* (Monarch/Administry, 2001), Paul Goodliff, *Pastoral Care in a Confused Climate* (DLT, 1998), Eddie Gibbs, *Church Next* (IVP, 2000), John Drane,

The McDonaldization of the Church (DLT, 2000), Thomas Hawkins, *The Learning Congregation* (John Knox, 1997), Alan Nelson, *Leading Your Ministry* (Abingdon Press, 1996).

9. For the latest details on Church Growth and Decline in the United Kingdom see Peter Brierley, *The Tide is Running Out* (Christian Research Association, 2000).

10. Paul Goodliff, *Pastoral Care in a Confused Climate*, p. 57.

11. For research on how moving home is likely to affect church attendance see Philip Richter and Leslie Francis, *Gone but not Forgotten – Church Leaving and Returning* (DLT, 1998), pp. 65–75.

12. As early as 1993, before widespread Sunday trading, 3 per cent of people in one survey claimed that they stopped attending church because of work patterns (Michael Fanstone, *The Sheep that Got Away*, Monarch, 1993, p. 63).

13. In *The Tide is Running Out*, Peter Brierley reports that the Church in the UK 'were losing 500 children under 15 in the 1980s and that has now doubled to a net outturn of 1,000 boys and girls every week', pp. 110ff.

14. Source: unpublished research carried out by the Dioceses of Wakefield and Ripon in 1999 and available from the Diocesan offices. A summary of the findings can be found in the report *Statistics A Tool for Mission*, A Report by the Statistics Review Group (Church House Publishing, 2000). The Wakefield report found the core congregation (attending at least 6 weeks out of 8) to be just 17 per cent of the total pool who came to church. Fifty-two per cent of attenders came just one Sunday out of 8. See also Brierley, *The Tide is Running Out*, p. 73.

15. Brierley, *The Tide is Running Out*, pp. 109f.

16. Source: Mark Ireland, unpublished MA dissertation (Cliff College, 2000). At the time of writing the research can be consulted at www.lichfield.anglican.org.

17. For a summary of the present position in the Church of England see the article 'Adult education and formal lay ministries' by Mrs Hilary Ineson and Revd Ian Stubbs in *Ministry Issues for the Church of England* by Gordon W. Kuhrt (Church House Publishing, 2001), pp. 124–31.

18. Brierley, *The Tide is Running Out*, p. 56.

19. *ibid.*, pp. 34 and 37.

20. *ibid.*, p. 51.

21. For a concise and encouraging overview of practical responses to declining church attendance see 'There are Answers', Springboard Resource Paper 1, by Robert Warren and Bob Jackson (Springboard, 2001).

22. Martyn Percy has recently published a series of essays which attempt to challenge the strong hold on the churches of the secularisation thesis: that our society is becoming steadily less religious: Martyn Percy, *The Salt of the Earth, Religious Resilience in a Secular Age* (Continuum/ Sheffield Academic Press, 2001); for a recent and full statement of this thesis see Callum Brown, *The Death of Christian Britain: Understanding*

Secularisation, 1800–2000 (Routledge, 2000).

23. For a detailed analysis see Jan Kerkhofs (ed.), *Europe without Priests* (SCM, 1995), especially Chapter 1.

24. In 'The parish system' published in *Ministry Issues for the Church of England* by Gordon W. Kuhrt, pp. 213–4.

25. Percy, *Salt of the Earth, Religious Resilience in a Secular Age*, p. 340.

26. See *Ministry Issues for the Church of England* by Gordon W. Kuhrt, chapters 5–8, for an overview of developments since 1960; and 'Shaping Ministry for a Missionary Church' (ABM Ministry Paper 18) for a review of diocesan ministry strategy documents.

27. Gordon W. Kuhrt, *Ministry Issues for the Church of England*, p. 77.

28. One interesting structural observation made to me in response to an early draft by Philip King, former Secretary of the General Synod Board of Mission, is that new thinking about church 'falls between the stools for Ministry, Mission and Education' both in the central structures and in Anglican dioceses (letter to the author, 16 January 2002).

3. Renewing Vision

1. 2 Kings 21:1–18.
2. 2 Kings 22:11.
3. 2 Kings 23:3.
4. 2 Kings 23:22.
5. For a summary of organisational thinking on vision as part of leadership see Richard Daft, *Leadership Theory and Practice* (The Dryden Press, 1999), Part Three, pp. 121–51. For the Christian perspective see Peter Brierley, *Vision Building* (Hodder and Stoughton, 1989); John Finney, *Understanding Leadership* (Daybreak, 1989), pp. 114–32; David Pytches, *Leadership for New Life* (Hodder and Stoughton, 1998), pp. 54–62; Walter C. Wright, *Relational Leadership* (Paternoster, 2000), pp. 62–103; John Leach, *Visionary Leadership in the Local Church* (Grove Pastoral Series 72, Grove Books, 1997).
6. For materials to help in Mission Audit see *Faith in the City* (CHP, 1985), Appendix A, pp. 367ff.; and John Finney, *The Well Church Book* (CPAS/SU, 1991). New material is currently under preparation by Churches Together in Britain and Ireland.
7. Report from the *Halifax Guardian*, Monday 20 October, 1911, of the speech by the Rev. I. Parkinson to the Old Scholars' Re-union at St George's, Lee Mount, reprinted in *Early Reminiscences of St George's Church, Ovenden, Halifax,* compiled in 1914 but not published until 1923.
8. Andrew J. DuBrin, *The Complete Idiot's Guide to Leadership*, Second Edition (Alpha Books, Macmillan USA, 2000), panel inside front cover.
9. Numbers 22; 2 Kings 6:8–19; Luke 8:10; Matthew 16:13–20; Luke 24:13–35.
10. In *The Complete Idiot's Guide to Leadership* (p. 140) Andrew Dubrin defines vision as 'An idealised scenario of what the future can be for your organisation or organisational unit'.

11. 'For organisations, a vision is an attractive, ideal future that is credible yet not readily attainable. A vision is not just a dream – it is an ambitious view of the future that everyone in the organisation can believe in, one that can realistically be achieved, yet offers a future that is better in important ways that what now exists … For example Coca Cola's: "A Coke within arm's reach for everyone on the planet"', Richard Daft in *Leadership Theory and Practice* (Dryden Press, 1999), p. 126. For a discussion of the vocabulary of management from a different Christian perspective see Stephen Pattison, *The faith of the managers – when management becomes religion* (Cassell, 1997), Chapter 4, 'Words and Worlds', pp. 59–73. Pattison is wrong, in my view, to restrict the biblical concept of vision to prophetic visions and to describe it as the product of 'religious fanaticism' (p. 73). The idea of seeing clearly is a much richer, mainstream biblical theme.

13. Deuteronomy 1:33. See Leach, *Visionary Leadership in the Local Church*, pp. 12ff., for an expansion of this theme.

14. 2 Samuel 24.

15. 1 Samuel 16:7 at the anointing of David is the classic text: 'Do not look on his appearance or on the height of his stature, because I have rejected him; for the Lord does not see as mortals see; they look on the outward appearance, but the Lord looks on the heart.' For the critique of the nation see especially the criticism levelled by Elijah and Elisha at the Omride dynasty in 1 Kings 17ff. The dynasty is outwardly successful but inwardly corrupt.

16. Amos 5:23–4. For the identical concept applied to both individuals and communities see Jesus' penetrating critique of outward observance and inner reality in Matthew 5:21–42 and Matthew 23:1–36.

17. Matthew 16:24–6.

18. Isaiah 42:3.

19. Psalm 23 and the hymn 'Father, hear the prayer we offer', verse 3, Mission Praise 132, combined words edition (Marshall Pickering, 1999).

20. John 15:1–3.

21. For a discussion of the Council see Ben Witherington III, *The Acts of the Apostles – A social-rhetorical commentary* (Eerdmans/Paternoster, 1998) and Steven Croft, *Missionary Journeys–Missionary Church* (Emmaus Bible Resources 2, National Society/Church House Publishing, 2001), Chapter 2.

22. Acts 15:28.

23. The church can therefore in this sense be seen as a learning organisation. See Peter M. Senge, *The Fifth Discipline: The Art and Practice of the Learning Organisation* (Doubleday/Currency Books, 1990) and Thomas Hawkins, *The Learning Congregation* (John Knox, 1997).

24. See, for example, Daft, *Leadership Theory and Practice*, pp. 152–72; Dubrin, *The Complete Idiot's Guide to Leadership*, pp. 55–69. Communication is recognised throughout the literature as a hugely important part of the task of leadership.

25. For an excellent discussion of this variety in communication see John Drane, *The McDonaldization of the Church* (DLT, 2000), Chapter 6, 'Prophetic Gifts', pp. 112–32.

4. Models for the Future?

1. 1 Kings 12:4.
2. 1 Kings 12:7.
3. The concepts of 'servant' and of leadership are, of course, closely connected in the biblical tradition, in the churches' understanding of ordination and, recently, in contemporary literature about leadership. For the former see *Ministry in Three Dimensions* (DLT, 1999), pp. 45–59, and Walter C. Wright, *Relational Leadership* (Paternoster, 2000), pp. 1–21; for the latter see Robert Greanleaf, *Servant Leadership* (Paulist Press, 1977) and Richard Daft, *Leadership Theory and Practice* (Dryden Press, 1999), pp. 374–77.
4. 1 Kings 12:10–12. A scorpion seems to have been a more vicious form of whip.
5. *Shaping Ministry for a Missionary Church*, ABM Ministry Paper 18, 1998; reviewed and summarised in *Ministry Issues for the Church of England* by Gordon W. Kuhrt (CHP, 2001), pp. 61f.
6. It is important to say explicitly at this point that I would want to affirm collaborative ministry as a whole and the insights of the local ministry movement in particular (as represented by Robin Greenwood, Andrew Bowden and Michael West and others). Much detailed and excellent work has been done in order to enable shared patterns of ministry. The best of this thinking, represented by these authors, is also moving towards new ways and patterns of being church. The weakness of this approach, however, is that if we need to find a new way of being church then our starting point must be broader than reflection on ministry. See Robin Greenwood, *Transforming Church* (SPCK, 2002) and Andrew Bowden and Michael West, *Dynamic Local Ministry* (Continuum, 2001).
7. Arlin Rothauge, *Sizing up a congregation for new member ministry* (The Episcopal Church Center). A description of the basic church types referred to here is given in Appendix 2 of *Ministry in Three Dimensions*, pp. 194–99, and in a different form in Malcolm Grundy, *Understanding Congregations* (Mowbray, 1998), Chapter 2.
8. For a fuller description of current church sizes in England see Brierley, *The Tide is Running Out* (Christian Research Association, 2000), pp. 47ff.
9. Figures derived or quoted from Brierley, *The Tide is Running Out*, pp. 47–50. All numbers refer to adults and children in church on Sundays with each person counted only once (even if they come to more than one service).
10. The main raw material for these observations is the experience of analysing church attendance statistics in the Diocese of Wakefield for the six years from 1990 to 1996, supported by continued observation of patterns of church attendance growth and decline connected to pastoral

re-organisation.

11. The classic text for the UK is Eddie Gibbs, *I Believe in Church Growth* (Hodder and Stoughton, 1981).

12. For a description of Willow Creek see Lynne and Bill Hybels, *Rediscovering Church* (HarperCollins, 1996).

13. John Wimber, *Power Evangelism* (Hodder and Stoughton, 1985) and *Power Healing* (Hodder and Stoughton, 1986).

14. Ralph Neighbour, *Where do we go from here* (Touch Publications, 1991); William Beckham, *The Second Reformation* (Touch Publications, 1975); Howard Astin, *Body and Cell* (Monarch, 1998).

15. Rick Warren, *The Purpose Driven Church* (Zondervan, 1995).

16. For a discussion of this see Mark Noll, *The Scandal of the Evangelical Mind* (Eerdmans, 1994).

17. Cursillo is Spanish for 'Little Course'. The movement is one for spiritual renewal which has been growing for some time and is now operating in many Anglican dioceses in the UK.

18. The Roman Catholic Rite for the Christian Initiation of Adults, see Christine Dodd, *Making RCIA work* (Geoffrey Chapman, 1993).

19. John Drane, *The McDonaldization of the Church* (DLT, 2000). See also, Stephen Pattison, 'Some Objections to Aims and Objectives', in G.R. Evans and Martyn Percy (eds.), *Managing the Church? Order and Organisation in a Secular Age* (Lincoln Studies in Religion and Society 1, Sheffield Academic Press, 2000).

20. George Ritzer, *The McDonaldisation of Society* (Pine Forge Press, 1993).

21. Hybels, *Rediscovering Church*, p. 169.

22. Revelation 2–3.

23. Genesis 1:28, The Marriage Service, *Common Worship*, Pastoral Services (Church House Publishing, 2000), p. 105.

24. Ralph Neighbour, *Where do we go from here* (Touch Publications, 1990), p. 238.

25. Christian Schwartz, *Natural Church Development* (British Church Growth Association, 1997) and *Paridigm Shift in the Church – How Natural Church Development can transform Theological Thinking* (Churchsmart Resources, 1999).

26. *Growing Healthy Churches* – leaflet published by Springboard, 2001.

27. Mark 8:35.

28. Michael Moynagh, *Changing World, Changing Church* (Monarch/Administry, 2001); Eddie Gibbs and Ian Coffey, *Church Next, Quantum Changes in Christian Ministry* (IVP, 2001).

29. Robin Greenwood, *Transforming Church, Liberating Structures for Ministry* (SPCK, 2002).

5. A Way Forward?

1. Deuteronomy 1:19–45 retelling the longer account given in Numbers 13 and 14.

2. Deuteronomy 1:9–18 retelling the longer account given in Exodus 18.

3. Deuteronomy 1:9–12. See also the graphic account of the people queuing from morning until night in Exodus 18:13–18.

4. From earliest times both Jewish and Christian commentators have debated Jethro's role as a non-Israelite in the bringing of new insights to the life of the people of God. The passage has been used as a strong justification for the Church being open to insights from those of other faiths and, more recently, to secular wisdom. See the discussion in Brevard Childs, *Exodus* (SCM Press, 1974), pp. 332–36; *Ancient Christian Commentary on Scripture, Old Testament III*, edited by Joseph T. Lienhard (IVP, 2001), pp. 93–4.

5. Deuteronomy 1:15.

6. Exodus 18:20.

7. Luke 6:12–16; Acts 1:15–26.

8. See, for example, Carl George, *Prepare your Church for the Future* (Revell, 1991), pp. 121–25, and *The Coming Church Revolution* (Revell, 1994), pp. 54–61.

9. It can no longer be assumed that the leaders in either urban and rural societies will also assume positions of responsibility in the life of the local church as was once the case.

10. Robert Warren, *Building Missionary Congregations* (Church House Publishing, 1995), pp. 35f.

11. Acts 2:1–13, 46; 16:13; 19:9; 20:20.

12. More is said about these ministry teams in Part Three.

6. Foundations, Roots and Resources

1. Mark 3:13–14 NIV.

2. Mark 8:34.

3. Romans 12:1.

4. Romans 6:3–4.

5. *Baptism, Eucharist and Ministry* (World Council of Churches, 1982), p. 4.

6. From the Service of Baptism of those able to answer in *The Methodist Worship Book* (Methodist Publishing House, 1999), p. 85. For the parallel passage in the Church of England Service see *Common Worship* (Church House Publishing, 2000), p. 359.

7. From the Methodist Covenant Service in *The Methodist Worship Book*, p. 290.

8. For more on this theme see David Bosch, *Transforming Mission* (Orbis, 1991), pp. 467–74; Hans Kung, *The Church* (Burns and Oates, 1968), pp. 370–87; *Called to Love and Praise*, The Methodist Church Faith and Order Committee (1995), pp. 42–4; Thomas F. Torrance, 'Service in Jesus Christ' in *Theological Foundations for Ministry*, ed. R. S. Anderson (T & T Clark, 1979) pp. 714–33; Jurgen Moltmann, *The Church in the Power of the Spirit* (SCM, 1977), IV, 'The Church and the Kingdom of God', pp. 133–97.

9. In Matthew, the kingdom of heaven. See Mark 1:15; 4:11; Matthew 13:1–50; Luke 6:20; 10:9, etc.

10. Matthew 16:18 and 18:17.
11. For more on the kingdom of God see, for example, J. Andrew Kirk, *What is Mission* (DLT, 1999), Chapter 3, and David Bosch, *Transforming Mission* (Orbis, 1993), Chapter 1; Jurgen Moltmann, *The Church in the Power of the Spirit* (SCM, 1977), Section IV; Kevin Giles, *What on earth is the Church* (SPCK, 1995), Chapter 2.
12. For a full discussion of mission within the horizon of the kingdom of God see Kirk, *What is Mission,* and Bosch, *Transforming Mission.*
13. Mark 12:28–31.
14. Mark 3:14.
15. Even in the instances where Jesus is dealing with thousands of people, there is evidence of him dividing up the very large groups into smaller units in order to develop and sustain manageable community – see Mark 6:40.
16. Mark 1:14.
17. Acts 2:45–6.
18. Acts 20:20.
19. For further evidence of this practice in Acts see Acts 16:15 and 40, where Lydia's home becomes the base for the first church there; Acts 20:7ff., where Paul addresses a small community in Troas in an upper room, and Acts 28:30, the last scene of the book, which describes Paul imprisoned in Rome but using his place of confinement as a place of hospitality, teaching and Christian community. In the Epistles we read on several occasions of a church being described by the place where it meets: Romans 16:5 – 'Greet also the church in their house' (that is Prisca and Aquila); 1 Corinthians 16:19 – 'Aquila and Prisca, together with the church in their house greet you warmly in the Lord'; Colossians 4:15 – 'Give my greetings to the brothers and sisters in Laodicea, and to Nympha and the church in her house'; and Philemon – 2 – 'To Philemon our dear friend and co-worker, to Apphia our sister, to Archippus our fellow-soldier and to the church in your house'.
20. For more on this see Wayne Meeks, *The First Urban Christians, The Social World of the Apostle Paul* (Yale University Press, 1983).
21. For an alternative overview of sources see Robert and Julia Banks, *The Church Comes Home, Building Community and Mission through Home Churches* (Hendrickson Publishers, 1998), Chapter 3.
22. The rule itself dates from the sixth century, draws on earlier rules and inspired most of the later guides to the monastic life. The most accessible translation and commentary is that of Esther de Waal, *A Life Giving Way, A commentary on the rule of St. Benedict* (Geoffrey Chapman, 1995). For a more general introduction to Benedictine spirituality see Esther de Waal, *Seeking God* (Fount, 1984 and 1996).
23. See Bede, *Ecclesiastical History of the English People,* translated by Leo Shirley-Price (Penguin Books, 1955).
24. Martin Luther, Preface to The German Mass and Orders of Service, in Luther's *Works,* vol. 53, gen. ed. Helmut T. Lehmann, tr. Paul Zeller

(Fortress Press, 1965), pp. 63–4; quoted with comments by William A. Beckham, *The Second Reformation, Reshaping the Church for the 21st Century*, pp. 115f.

25. First published in 1656. Available today as a Banner of Truth Publication.

26. For the story of the emergence of Methodism see Davies and Rupp, *A History of the Methodist Church in Great Britain*, Volume One (1965); Henry D. Rack, *Reasonable Enthusiast, John Wesley and Rise of Methodism* (Epworth Press, 1992), especially pp. 237ff.; D. Henderson, *John Wesley's Class Meetings – a model for making disciples* (Evangel/Francis Asbury, 1997); Paul Worsnop, *Facilitating Mission in British Methodist Churches, Lessons from historical and contemporary models*, MA thesis (University of Durham, 2000), Chapter Two.

27. The Methodist Church Faith and Order Committee, *Called to Love and Praise*, Report to Conference (1995), 4.3.5, p. 36.

28. *From Mark Smith, Religion in Industrial Society, Oldham and Saddleworth, 1740–1865*, Oxford Historical Monographs (Clarendon Press, 1994), p.149 quoting the LCBA Circular letter (1862). Smith comments elsewhere (p. 232) that in the 1840s all of the evangelical churches in the Oldham and Saddleworth area, Anglican and non-conformist, were employing very similar pastoral and evangelistic strategies, including cottage meetings.

29. The most influential literature on small groups in the church in the 1970s and 1980s was a series of books by John Mallison, *Building Small Groups in the Christian Community* and *Creative Ideas for Small Groups in the Christian Community* (SU, 1978). Mallison's work remains both credible and readable and certainly contains a mission emphasis which was only seldom taken up in churches in the UK. A second set of influential material was the Serendipity Series produced by Lyman Coleman for both adults and young people (main book SU, 1982). Serendipity encourages open groups and an empty chair as a symbol of this but mission is not part of the group's agenda, which focuses instead on becoming a supportive Christian community, personal growth, spiritual gifts, spiritual wholeness and celebration (*Search the Scriptures*, SU, 1980, p. 5).

30. See Margaret Hebblethwaite, *Base Communities – An Introduction* (Geoffrey Chapman, 1993); Leonardo Boff, *Church, Charism and Power* (SCM Press, 1981), especially chapters 9 and 10; David Prior, *The Church in the Home* (Marshall, Morgan and Scott, 1983). A limited amount of resourcing of base ecclesial communities in the UK has been undertaken by USPG and the network New Way Publications (25, Taylor Avenue, Kew, Surrey, TW9 4EB).

31. The basic bibliography for the Cell Church movement in the UK is provided by the larger texts of Ralph Neighbour, *Where do we go from here* (Touch Publications, 1991) and William Beckham, *The Second Reformation* (Touch Publications, 1995). The main British publications to

date are Howard Astin, *Body and Cell* (Monarch, 1998) and Phil Potter, *The Challenge of Cell Church* (BRF and CPAS, 2001). The organisation YWAM hosts and leads Cell Church conferences with Neighbour and Beckham as speakers. CPAS have been influential in promoting this new way of being church. The Church Army's Sheffield Centre keeps a resource of research and publications on the movement; Anglican Church Planting Initiatives maintain a database and provide consultancy for churches seeking to develop their life in this way. A similar and related adaptation of Cell Church ideas is provided by Carl George with his concept of the Metachurch. George is the latest in a distinguished line of Church Growth consultants based at Fuller: Peter Wagner; John Wimber; Eddie Gibbs. The Metachurch concept is based upon the concept of nurturing both congregation and small group. Its slogan is: 'Large enough to celebrate, small enough to care'; see Carl George, *The Coming Church Revolution* (Revell, 1994) (Cell Church and Metachurch writers are not given to modesty in their book titles).

32. Particularly the *Return of the Prodigal Son* (DLT, 1994).
33. Jean Vanier, *Community and Growth*, Revised Edition (DLT, 1989).
34. Bishop Michael Turnbull in a letter to the author, 28 February 2002.

Part Three: NURTURING THE VISION: THE CHURCH IN SCRIPTURE AND TRADITION

Introduction

1. C.S. Lewis, *The Screwtape Letters* (Unwin Brothers, 19), Letter II, p. 42.
2. The Second Letter of John uses the image of the 'elect lady' as an image for the church to which the author is writing.

7. The Called Community: The Church in Relationship with God

1. 1 Peter 2:9–10.
2. 1 Peter 1:6.
3. For a full discussion of the term *ekklesia* and a very thorough discussion of the concept of the Church in the New Testament see Kevin Giles, *What on Earth is the Church? A Biblical and Theological Enquiry* (SPCK, 1995).
4. Genesis 12:1.
5. Genesis 12:3.
6. Exodus 6:7, cf. Deuteronomy 4:20; 2 Samuel 7:24; Jeremiah 13:11.
7. Deuteronomy 4:32–4.
8. Jeremiah 31:33–4.
9. See, for example, Genesis 12:3; Exodus 19:6 (where the concept of Israel as a nation of priests to the nations is introduced); Psalms 67 and 96 among others; and Isaiah 49:1–6 where Israel is called to be a light to the nations. For further material on this theme see Walter C. Kaiser Jr, *The Mission of God in the Old Testament* (Baker Books, 2000). For a contemporary outworking of this theme from an Old Testament text see Raymond

Fung, *The Isaiah Vision* (WCC Publications, 1993). The Book of Jonah should be read as a parable about Israel's reluctance to fulfil her particular vocation to speak of God among the nations. As such, the story remains of striking contemporary relevance: see Eugene Peterson, *Under the Unpredictable Plant, an exploration in vocational holiness* (Eerdmans, 1992).

10. Joel 2:28–9, verses quoted by Peter on the day of Pentecost according to Acts 2:17ff.

11. Romans 11:17–18. For a fuller exploration of these roots, see Hans Kung, *The Church* (Burns and Oates, 1968), pp. 114–25; Jurgen Moltmann, *The Church in the Power of the Spirit* (SCM, 1977), pp. 136–50.

12. Recent studies of the Gospel of Matthew have drawn attention to Matthew's emphasis on discipleship and the need to make disciples even among those who may be already part of the Christian community. The commission at the end of the Gospel itself shapes the telling of the story of Jesus and his disciples: on every page we are given lessons about disciple making. See, for example, David Bosch, *Transforming Mission* (Orbis, 1991), pp. 56–74: 'In Matthew's understanding the church is only to be found where disciples live in community with one another and their Lord and where they seek to live according to "the will of the Father"' (p. 83).

13. Mark 1:14–20.

14. Mark 3:14.

15. Luke 5:1–11.

16. Matthew 9:9–10.

17. Matthew 16:18.

18. Matthew 18:17.

19. A. Loisy, *L'Evanglile et L'Eglise* (Paris, 1902), p. 111 as quoted in Kung, *The Church*, p. 43. Kung adds the comment: 'This quotation is always taken in the wrong, i.e. a negative sense; Loisy meant it as a positive statement.'

20. 'Someone told him, "Look, your mother and your brothers are standing outside, wanting to speak to you." But to the one who had told him this, Jesus replied, "Who is my mother and who are my brothers?" And pointing to his disciples, he said, "Here are my mother and my brothers. For whoever does the will of my Father in heaven is my brother and sister and mother"' (Matthew 12:48–50).

21. See 1 Corinthians 10:1–22.

22. Galatians 5:22–6; Ephesians 1:13–14; Romans 8.

23. Acts 4:23–31.

24. See above p. 91.

25. Ephesians 1:6, 12, 14.

26. 1 Peter 2:9. The term 'priesthood' used here itself implies a sense of mission: there is a wider community among whom we are called to be priests.

27. Revelation 21:22f.

28. Matthew 5:13f.
29. Romans 8:19.
30. See especially Hosea 1–3 but also Isaiah 54:1–8; Isaiah 62:4; Jeremiah 3 and Ezekiel 16.
31. Matthew 22:1–13 and Matthew 25:1–13.
32. 2 Corinthians 11:2. See also Ephesians 5:32.
33. Revelation 19:7–9.
34. For more on the Church as the Bride of Christ see R. Batey, *New Testament Nuptial Imagery* (E.J. Brill, 1971); David Watson, *I Believe in the Church* (Hodder and Stoughton, 1978), pp. 129–40.
35. The most important and widely used text is John D. Zizioulas, *Being as Communion, Studies in Personhood and the Church* (St Vladimir's University Press, 1985). Zizioulas' work has helped the whole Church recover the doctrine of the Trinity as developed by the Cappadocian Fathers and preserved within the Orthodox tradition.
36. For a very detailed and significant outworking of this see Robin Greenwood, *Transforming Priesthood, A New Theology of Mission and Ministry* (SPCK, 1994).
37. These themes run all through the service but are focused in the great prayer of thanksgiving where the preface, the first part of the prayer, gives thanks for the grace of God, Father, Son and Holy Spirit, in creation, redemption and the gift of God's presence.
38. Again, recent themes in ecclesiology have emphasised the close link between understanding the doctrine of the church and that of the sacraments: see Robert Jenson, *The Church and the Sacraments*.
39. From the charge to priests in the ASB Ordinal, *The Alternative Services Book 1980*, p. 357.
40. The reasons for this are complex. For a thorough analysis from an American perspective see Robert Putnam, *Bowling Alone: The Collapse and Revival of American Community* (Simon and Schuster, 1999).

8. Members of One Body: The Church in Relation to Herself

1. Words at the Introduction to the Peace from *Common Worship, Services and Prayers for the Church of England* (Church House Publishing, 2000), p. 290.
2. Mark 3:21–4.
3. Mark 3:31–5.
4. Mark 9:33–7 and 10:35–45.
5. Matthew 5–7; 10; 13; 18 and 23. Matthew is the most Jewish of the Gospel writers and commentators have compared these five great collections of teaching with the five books of the law.
6. Matthew 16:18–19.
7. Matthew 18:6–7.
8. Matthew 18:15–17. The phrases 'member of the church' and 'member' here are the way the NRSV translates and interprets the Greek word *adelphos*, which means, literally, 'your brother'.

9. Matthew 18:21–2. Again, the phrase 'member of the church' translates 'brother'.

10. See, for example, Luke 14:7–24.

11. For a more detailed exposition of Luke 24 see Steven Croft, *The Lord is Risen!* (Emmaus Bible Resources 1, Church House Publishing, 2001).

12. Acts 1:15–26.

13. Acts 2:42–7.

14. Acts 4:32–5.

15. Acts 6:1–7; 13:1–3 and 14:23.

16. See, for example, Acts 16:11–40 for the account of the church at Philippi; Acts 20:7–12 for Paul's farewell visit to Troas and Acts 20:36 for the close bonds of Christian love between Paul and the elders in the church at Ephesus. For more on this theme see Steven Croft, *Missionary Journeys – Missionary Church* (Emmaus Bible Resources 2, Church House Publishing, 2001).

17. For an excellent discussion of this see David Seccombe, 'Luke's Vision for the Church' in *A Vision for the Church: Studies in Early Christian Ecclesiology in honour of J.P.M. Swete*, edited by Markus Bockmuehl and Michael Thompson (T & T Clarke, 1997), pp. 53f. Seccombe points out that Luke deliberately avoids using the term *ekklesia* in the Acts narrative until he slips it in as an incidental reference in Acts 5:11. Thereafter, he gives the term a theological identity through the speech of Stephen, connecting the church to the *ekklesia* of Israel and thereafter uses it freely but only to refer to individual Christian communities rather than the Church throughout the world.

18. John 10:16.

19. John 13:14–15.

20. John 13:34–5, cf. John 15:12f.

21. John 17:20–3.

22. Romans 12:4–8; 1 Corinthians 10:14–17 and 12:12–31; Ephesians 1:22–3; 2:16; 4:4–16; Colossians 1:15, 18, 24; 2:19; 3:15. Of these, the first two are undoubtedly Pauline. Ephesians and Colossians are thought to represent either a later stage in Paul's thought or the work of a different author.

23. James D.G. Dunn, *The Theology of Paul the Apostle* (T & T Clark, 1998), pp. 548ff. The classical fable of Menenius Agrippa which uses the image in a similar way to Paul is quoted on p. 550. See also Hans Kung, *The Church* (Burns and Oates, 1968), pp. 203–63; Lesslie Newbigin, *The Household of God* (SCM, 1953, reprinted by Paternoster Press, 1998), pp. 72–111, and David Watson, *I believe in the Church* (Hodder and Stoughton, 1978), pp. 96–115.

24. 1 Corinthians 12:27 NIV.

25. Romans 12:4–5 NIV.

26. Colossians 1:18 NIV. See also Colossians 1:24.

27. Ephesians 1:22–3 NIV, cf. 2:16 where there appears to be a double meaning on the phrase 'body of Christ': the body of Christ through

which men and women were reconciled by his death on the cross and the body of Christ into which people are brought through this reconciliation; and 3:6 where the Jews and Christians together are included in this one body.

28. Ephesians 4:4 NIV.
29. Ephesians 4:12–13 NIV.
30. Ephesians 4:16 NIV. The image recurs in Ephesians 5:30, linked with that of the bride.
31. 1 Corinthians 12:26.
32. Romans 12:15–16.
33. To trace the story see Eric G. Jay, *The Church: its changing image through twenty centuries,* 2 volumes (SPCK, 1977).
34. These four are often described as the marks of the church. The word 'catholic' here is taken from the Greek word *katholice* and describes the Church throughout the whole world rather than simply the Roman Catholic Church. The standard ecclesiologies contain a detailed discussion of these four great marks of the Christian Church. See, for example, Kung, *The Church,* pp. 263–363; Jurgen Moltmann, *The Church in the Power of the Spirit* (SCM, 1997), pp. 337–62, Alister McGrath, *Christian Theology, An Introduction,* Second Edition (Blackwell, 1994), pp. 482–92.
35. See especially the important report, *Working as One Body,* the Archbishops' Commission on the Structures of the Church of England where the Body image provides the sole theological undergirding for the reforms leading the establishing of the Archbishops' Council.
36. David Hope, 'Changing Church, Unchanging God', Sermon to the University of Cambridge, 4 February, 2001, in *Signs of Hope* (Continuum, 2001), pp. 139–49.
37. For the classical description of these see Avery Dulles, *Models of the Church* (Gill and MacMillan, 1976). The five models Dulles describes are the Church as Institution, Mystical Communion, Sacrament, Herald and Servant.
38. Principally 1 Corinthians 12:27: 'You are the body of Christ'; and Ephesians 4:4–6.

9. A Light to the Nations: The Church in Relation to God's World
1. Matthew 5:14–15.
2. Genesis 1:3–4 and Revelation 22:5. For more on this general theme see the article on light in the *Dictionary of Biblical Imagery,* edited by Leland Ryken, James C. Wilhoit and Tremper Longman III (IVP, 1998), pp. 509–12.
3. Isaiah 42:6–7; cf. Isaiah 9:2; 49:6; 60:1–3.
4. Luke 1:78–9.
5. Luke 2:32.
6. See for example John 1:9; 8:12.
7. Luke 3:22.
8. Luke 4:18–19 quoting Isaiah 61:1–2.
9. Luke 5:10.

10. Luke 9:1–2.
11. Luke 10:2, cf. Luke 10:9.
12. Many good things have been written in recent decades about the Christian theology of mission which have not yet worked their way into the life of the church and the churches' own self-understanding. For an accessible and recent introduction to the subject see J. Andrew Kirk, *What is Mission? Theological Explorations* (Darton, Longman and Todd, 1999). The major work is David J. Bosch, *Transforming Mission: Paradigm Shifts in Theology of Mission* (Orbis, 1991).
13. Matthew 28:18–20.
14. For a recent overview of the different ways in which the Church has engaged with culture (and continues to do so) see 'Resistance and Accommodation: Theology and Contemporary Culture' in *Salt of the Earth: Religious Resilience in a Secular Age* by Martyn Percy, (Continuum/Sheffield Academic Press, 2002), pp. 36–60.
15. For one such process model of evangelism, nurture and Christian growth see *Emmaus: the way of faith* by Stephen Cottrell, Steven Croft, John Finney, Felicity Lawson, and Robert Warren (Church House Publishing, 1996 and 1998).
16. Holy Communion, *Common Worship* Order One (Church House Publishing, 2000), p. 179.
17. For an introductory exposition and bibliography see Avery Dulles, *Models of the Church* (Gill and MacMillan, 1976), Chapter IV, 'The Church as Sacrament', pp. 58–70.
18. Acts 2:1–4.
19. Ezekiel 37:1–14.
20. See, for example, Acts 4:31; 13:2; 19:1–6.
21. A church or group which wanted to explore this theme more fully might use the *Emmaus Growth Course, Come Holy Spirit* in *Knowing God, Emmaus Growth Courses Book 1* (NS/CHP, 1996).

10. Pilgrims in Progress: The Church in Relation to Time
1. The Epistle to Diognetus V, The Apostolic Fathers, from the American Edition of the *Ante Nicene Fathers*, Volume 1 (Hendrickson, 1999, original edition 1885), p. 26. The Epistle is an anonymous and very beautiful ancient Christian text, probably dating from the early second century.
2. It seems to me that seeing the Church through the lens of time and eternity has been a somewhat neglected dimension of ecclesiology in the literature. Recent studies look backwards to Scripture and Tradition and inwards (as it were) to the doctrine of the Trinity or the Body of Christ yet this is a continual theme of the New Testament.
3. Mark 1:15.
4. Matthew 6:10.
5. Matthew 13:24–33.
6. Matthew 20:1–16.
7. Matthew 25:1–13.

8. Matthew 25:14–30.
9. See especially Matthew 24:3–51; Mark 13:1–37; Luke 21:25–38.
10. Matthew 24:42.
11. Acts 1:6–11.
12. Romans 8:18–19, 22–4.
13. 1 Corinthians 13:12.
14. Revelation 21:1–2. The picture leads on to a much more detailed vision of the New Jerusalem, the Church, in vv. 9–27.
15. For more on the Church in Revelation see Kevin Giles, *What on Earth is the Church: a biblical and theological enquiry* (SPCK, 1995), p. 178.
16. Acts 9:2; 19:9; 19:23; 22:4; 24:14; 24:22; cf. John 14:6.
17. See for example Psalms 1, 25 etc.
18. See for example Hebrews 3 and 4 where the picture is used as an encouragement to an embattled community to persevere through difficulties to the promised rest of God.
19. 1 Peter 1:1, 17; 2:11.
20. Hebrews 11:13.
21. Ephesians 2:19.
22. The Epistle to Diognetus V and VI, The Apostolic Fathers, from the American Edition of the *Ante Nicene Fathers*, pp. 26 and 27.
23. Genesis 3:17–19.
24. Romans 8:18.
25. Ephesians 6:12–13.
26. Holy Baptism, *Common Worship* (Church House Publishing, 2000), p. 354.
27. Eucharistic Prayer B, Order One, Holy Communion, *Common Worship*, p. 190.
28. Eucharistic Prayer D, Order One, Holy Communion, *Common Worship*, p. 194.
29. Eucharistic Prayer F, Order One, Holy Communion, *Common Worship*, p. 200.
30. From Archbishop David Hope, 'Changing Church – Unchanging God': A sermon preached to the University of Cambridge, 4 February 2001, in *Signs of Hope* (Continuum, 2001), p. 144.

Part Four: ENABLING TRANSFORMING COMMUNITIES
11. Planning and Policies
1. See for example the Emmaus course on *Belonging to the Church*, Emmaus Growth Book Two (National Society/Church House Publishing 2001).
2. For literature on the establishing of such teams see Robin Greenwood, *Practising Community* (SPCK, 1999); *The Ministry Team Handbook* (SPCK, 2000); and *Transforming Church* (SPCK, 2002); Malcolm Grundy, *Understanding Congregations* (Mowbray, 1998), Chapter 4; and *Stranger in the Wings*, A Report on Local Non–Stipendiary Ministry (CHP, 1998).
3. F. Fukayama, *Trust, the Social Virtues and the Creation of Prosperity*

(Penguin, 1996) and Robert D. Putnam, *Bowling Alone: The Collapse and Revival of American Community* (Simon and Schuster, 2000).

4. *ibid.,* pp. 22f.
5. *ibid.,* p. 79.
6. Luke 14:12–14 NIV.
7. For more on developing healthy patterns of ministry and life for the ordained see the Rule of St Benedict, especially as interpreted by Esther de Waal in *A Life Giving Way: a commentary on the Rule of St. Benedict* (Geoffrey Chapman, 1995); Gordon MacDonald, *Ordering your Private World* (Highland, 1984); Chris Edmondson, *Fit to Lead: sustaining effective ministry in a changing world* (DLT, 2002).
8. The new series of Emmaus Bible Resources provides material for individual study, small group reflection and suggestions for linking the studies with Sunday worship through liturgy and series of sermons. Titles published so far are *The Lord is Risen!* on Luke 24 and *Missionary Journeys – Missionary Church* on Acts 13–20 (National Society/Church House Publishing, 2001). New titles on Jonah and Colossians are planned for November, 2002. The approach taken in the studies is ideally suited to the development of transforming communities.
9. Ralph Neighbour, *Where do we go from here?* (Touch Publications, 1990), p. 46.
10. Carl George, *Prepare Your Church for the Future* (Revell, 1994), p. 122.

12. Forming a Transforming Community

1. There is no study guide as such to this chapter, which is intended as basic training material and a manual for leaders of transforming communities. It should be possible to give an overview and then pause on each stage of the group's life for discussion, questions and feedback.
2. There is a wide range of literature on group and team building which attempts to describe the process by which a group becomes a community. For examples see Lyman Coleman, *Search the Scripture* (Serendipity House, 1983), p. 14; John Mallison, *Building Small Groups in the Christian Community* (Scripture Union, 1978); Stephen Cottrell *et al., The Emmaus Nurture Course* (CHP/NS, 1996) and *Leading an Emmaus Group* (National Society/CHP, 1998); Catherine Widdicombe, *Meetings that Work, A Practical Guide to Teamwork and Groups* (The Lutterworth Press, 1994, 2000); Jeanne Hinton, *Small and in Place: Practical Steps in Forming Small Christian Communities* (New Way Publications, 1998); for secular insights – which are remarkably similar – see Richard Daft, *Leadership Theory and Practice* (The Dryden Press, 1999), Chapter 10, 'Leading Teams'. A basic knowledge of how to see a small group of strangers grow into a community is a necessary part of every minister's toolkit.
3. The classic Cell Church material on the trajectory of cells can be found in Ralph Neighbour, *Where do we go from here?* (Touch Publications, 1990), pp. 236ff. It is well worth reading. The terms 'macro' and 'micro' are, I think, very useful and borrowed from Neighbour although I pre-

fer the word 'process' instead of 'trajectory', implying that there may be junctions and choices to be made along the way. Cell Church adaptations of Neighbour's work can be found in Howard Astin, *Body and Cell* (CPAS/Monarch, 1998), Chapter Three, and example outlines of meetings in Phil Potter, *The Challenge of Cell Church* (CPAS/BRF 2001).

4. For an example of the kinds of questions which may be helpful to facilitate sharing in this way see Potter, *The Challenge of Cell Church*, pp. 163f. Very good practical advice for this stage of the group's life can be found in Hinton, *Small and in Place, Practical Steps in Forming Small Christian Communities*, 1998.

5. The Emmaus Growth materials on Scripture, Prayer, Christian Identity, etc., will be useful here.

6. This area is somewhat under-resourced in terms of materials and literature. The excellent report 'Called to New Life: the world of lay discipleship' (NS/CHP, 1999) is a good beginning and contains a list of other resources.

7. Again, the Emmaus courses provide a great deal of useful and relevant material which can be used for the study section of the group's life at this point. *Living the Gospel*, in Growth Book 1, provides a simple four-session course on personal evangelism based upon the concept of *oikos* or household. The course was originally adapted from Cell Church material. *Called into Life* in Growth Book 4 is a five-session course on Christian vocation which contains very useful material for any group looking at these issues. The whole theme of Growth Book 4 is enabling the people of God in mission to the whole of life through two slightly longer courses on the beatitudes and the kingdom of God. Each growth course provides resources for prayer and suggestions for action. Each would need to be adapted to the specific stage in the life of the group (in other words it will generally be better to follow the broad outlines here for a two-hour meeting and borrow study, prayer and action resources as appropriate from the Emmaus materials). If the group prefers to study a continuous text then the second of the Emmaus Bible Resources, *Missionary Journeys – Missionary Church* (National Society/CHP, 2001) will be a helpful resource and, once again, is designed to lead the group into action together.

8. For practical ideas and very helpful insights into the way in which involvement in mission of this kind is transformative for all concerned, see Ann Morrisy, *Beyond the Good Samaritan: community, ministry and mission* (Mowbray, 1997).

9. Teaching the Christian faith to individuals and their immediate families has deep roots in the Christian tradition and in Anglican ministry. The classic text on the importance of the work is Richard Baxter's work, *The Reformed Pastor*, first published in 1656 (Banner of Truth, 1979). Those who want to explore this further will find a chapter in my earlier book, *Making New Disciples*, on the subject. The Cell Church movement has developed a whole set of materials for facilitating this process which are

useful as a model for adaptation to a different context.

10. An excellent range of resources for this kind of study has been developed by New Way Communities, 25, Taylor Avenue, Kew Surrey, TW9 4EB. See also Peter B. Price, *Seeds of the Word, Biblical Reflection for Small Church Communities* (DLT, 1996).

11. Carl George has this fascinating mathematical table of signal counts in small groups which gives some insight into why larger groups are more demanding to lead (Carl George, *Prepare your Church for the Future*, Revell, 1993, p. 127):

2 people	2 signals
3 people	9 signals
4 people	28 signals
5 people	75 signals
6 people	186 signals
7 people	441 signals
8 people	1,016 signals
9 people	2,295 signals
10 people	5,110 signals

Conclusion

1. Psalm 8:8–14, developing the image of God's people as a vineyard in Isaiah 5 and taken up in John 15.

Bibliography

Arbuckle, Gerald A. *Refounding the Church, Dissent for Leadership,* Geoffrey Chapman, 1993

Astin, Howard. *Body and Cell,* Monarch, 1998

Banks, Robert and Julia. *The Church Comes Home, Building Community and Mission through Home Churches,* Hendrickson Publishers, 1998

Barth, Karl. *Theology and Church,* Harper and Row, 1928

Beckham, William. *The Second Reformation,* Touch Publications, 1975

Bede. *Ecclesiastical History of the English People,* translated by Leo Shirley-Price, Penguin Books, 1955

Behrens, James. *Practical Church Management, A guide for every parish,* Gracewing, 1998

Bockmuehl, Markus and Thompson, Michael B. *A Vision for the Church – Studies in Early Christian Ecclesiology in honour of J.P.M. Swete,* T and T Clark, 1997

Boff, Leonardo. *Church, Charism and Power,* SCM Press, 1981

Bosch, David. *Transforming Mission,* Orbis, 1991

Bowden, Andrew and West, Michael. *Dynamic Local Ministry,* Continuum, 2000

Brierley, Peter. *The Tide is Running Out,* Christian Research Association, 2000
Vision Building, Hodder and Stoughton, 1989

Buchanan, Colin. *Is the Church of England Biblical? An Anglican Ecclesiology,* DLT, 1998

Childs, Brevard. *Exodus,* SCM Press, 1974

Coleman, Lyman. *Search the Scriptures,* Scripture Union, 1980

Cottrell, Stephen, Croft, Steven, Finney, John, Lawson, Felicity, and Warren, Robert. *Emmaus: the way of faith* (eight volumes), National Society/Church House Publishing, 1996 and 1998

Cottrell, Stephen and Croft, Steven. *Travelling Well: A companion guide to the Christian Faith,* NS/CHP 2000

Croft, Steven. *Growing New Christians,* CPAS/Marshall Pickering, 1993
Making New Disciples, Marshall Pickering, 1994
Man to Man, Friendship and Faith, SU, 1998
Ministry in Three Dimensions: Ordination and Leadership in the Local Church, DLT, 1999
Missionary Journeys – Missionary Church, Emmaus Bible Resources 2,

National Society/Church House Publishing, 2001

The Lord is Risen! Emmaus Bible Resources 1, Church House Publishing, 2001

Cueni, R. Robert. *Dinosaur Heart Transplants – Renewing Mainline Congregations*, Abingdon Press, 2000

Daft, Richard. *Leadership Theory and Practice*, The Dryden Press, 1999

de Waal, Esther. *Seeking God*, Fount, 1984 and 1996

A Life Giving Way, A commentary on the rule of St. Benedict, Geoffrey Chapman, 1995

Dodd, Christine. *Making RCIA work*, Geoffrey Chapman, 1993

Drane, John. *The McDonaldization of the Church*, DLT, 2000

DuBrin, Andrew J. *The Complete Idiot's Guide to Leadership*, Second Edition, Alpha Books, Macmillan USA, 2000

Dulles, Avery. *Models of the Church*, Gill and MacMillan, 1976

Dunn, James D.G. *The Theology of Paul the Apostle*, T & T Clark, 1998

Edmondson, Chris. *Minister – Love Thyself, sustaining Healthy Ministry*, Grove Pastoral Series 83, Grove Books, 2000

Fit to Lead: sustaining effective ministry in a changing world, DLT, 2002

Etchells, Ruth. *Set my people free – a lay challenge to the churches*, Fount, 1995

Evans G.R. and Percy, Martyn (eds.). *Managing the Church? Order and Organisation in a secular age*, Lincoln Studies in Religion and Society 1, Sheffield Academic Press, 2000

Fanstone, Michael. *The Sheep that Got Away*, Monarch, 1993

Finney, John. *Understanding Leadership*, Daybreak, 1989

The Well Church Book, CPAS/SU, 1991

Church on the Move – Leadership for Mission, Daybreak, 1992

Ford, David. *Self and Salvation, Being Transformed, Cambridge Studies in Christian Doctrine*, Cambridge University Press, 1999

Fukayama, F. *Trust, the Social Virtues and the Creation of Prosperity*, Penguin, 1996

Fung, Raymond. *The Isaiah Vision*, WCC Publications, 1993

General Synod. *Faith in the City*, Church House Publishing, 1984

Working as One Body: the Archbishops' Commission on the Structures of the Church of England, CHP, 1996

Shaping Ministry for a Missionary Church (ABM Ministry Paper 18), CHP, 1998

Stranger in the Wings, A report on Local Non-Stipendiary Ministry, CHP, 1998

Called to New Life: the world of lay discipleship, NS/CHP 1999

Statistics A Tool for Mission, A report by the Statistics Review Group, Church House Publishing, 2000

George, Carl. *Prepare your Church for the Future*, Revell, 1991

The Coming Church Revolution, Revell, 1994

How to break growth barriers, Revell, 1994

Gibbs, Eddie. *I Believe in Church Growth*, Hodder and Stoughton, 1981

Church Next, IVP, 2000

Gibbs, Eddie and Coffey, Ian. *Church Next, Quantum Changes in Christian Ministry*, IVP, 2001

Giles, Kevin. *What on Earth is the Church: a biblical and theological enquiry*, SPCK, 1995

Goodliff, Paul. *Pastoral Care in a Confused Climate*, DLT, 1998

Greanleaf, Robert. *Servant Leadership*, Paulist Press, 1977

Greenwood, Robin. *Transforming Priesthood, A New Theology of Mission and Ministry*, SPCK, 1994

  Practising Community, SPCK, 1999

  The Ministry Team Handbook, SPCK, 2000

  Transforming Church, SPCK, 2002

Grey, Mary C. *Beyond the Dark Night – A Way Forward for the Church?* Cassell, 1997

Grundy, Malcolm. *Understanding Congregations*, Mowbray, 1998

Hannaford, Robert. *A Church for the 21st Century – The Church of England Today and Tomorrow, An agenda for the future*, Gracewing, 1998

Hanson, A.T. and R.P.C. *The Identity of the Church – A guide to recognising the contemporary church*, SCM Press, 1987

Hardy, Daniel W. *Finding the Church – The Dynamic Truth of Anglicanism*, SCM Press, 2001

Hauerwas, Stanley. *In Good Company – The Church as Polis*, University of Notre Dame Press, 1995

Hawkins, Thomas. *The Learning Congregation*, John Knox, 1997

Hebblethwaite, Margaret. *Base Communities – An Introduction*, Geoffrey Chapman, 1993

Hemer, Colin J. *The Letters to the Seven Churches of Asia in their local setting*, Journal for the Study of New Testament Supplement Series 11, Sheffield Academic Press, 1986

Henderson, D. *John Wesley's Class Meetings – a model for making disciples*: Evangel/Francis Asbury, 1997

Hinton, Jeanne. *Small and in Place: Practical Steps in Forming Small Christian Communities*, New Way Publications, 1998

Hodgson, Janet and Warren, Robert. *Growing Healthy Churches*, Springboard, 2001

Hope, David. *Signs of Hope*, Continuum, 2001

Hunter, George G. III. *Leading and Managing a Growing Church*, Abingdon, 2000

Hybels, Lynne and Bill. *Rediscovering Church*, HarperCollins, 1996.

Ineson, Hilary and Stubbs, Ian. *Adult education and formal lay ministries* in Gordon W. Kuhrt, *Ministry Issues for the Church of England*, Church House Publishing, 2001

Jackman, David. *Understanding the Church*, Mentor, 1996

Kaiser, Walter C. Jr. *The Mission of God in the Old Testament*, Baker Books, 2000

Kerkhofs, Jan (ed.) *Europe without Priests?* SCM, 1995

Kirk, J. Andrew. *What is Mission*, DLT, 1999

Kuhrt, Gordon W. *Ministry Issues for the Church of England*, Church House Publishing, 2001

Kung, Hans. *The Church*, Burns and Oates, 1968

Leach, John. *Visionary Leadership in the Local Church*, Grove Pastoral Series 72, Grove Books, 1997

Lewis, C.S. *The Screwtape Letters*, Unwin Brothers, Letter II, p. 42

Lienhard, Joseph T. *Ancient Christian Commentary on Scripture, Old Testament III, Exodus-Deuteronomy*, IVP, 2001

Limouris, Gennadios. *Church, Kingdom, World – The Church as mystery and prophetic sign*, Faith and Order Papers 130, WCC, 1986

Lings, George. *Encounters on the Edge, Investigations from the Sheffield Centre*, available from The Sheffield Centre, 50 Cavendish Street, Sheffield, S3 7RZ

MacDonald, Gordon. *Ordering your Private World*, Highland, 1984

Mallison, John. *Building Small Groups in the Christian Community*, SU, 1978
Creative ideas for small groups in the Christian community, SU, 1978

Malphurs, Aubrey. *Advanced Strategic Planning – A new model for church and ministry leaders*, Baker Books, 1999

McGrath, Alister. *Christian Theology, An Introduction*, Second Edition, Blackwell, 1994

Meeks, Wayne. *The First Urban Christians, The Social World of the Apostle Paul*, Yale University Press, 1983

Moltmann, Jurgen. *The Church in the Power of the Spirit*, SCM, 1977

Morrisy, Ann. *Beyond the Good Samaritan: community, ministry and mission*, Mowbray, 1997

Moynagh, Michael. *Changing World, Changing Church*, Monarch, 2001

Nazir-Ali, Michael. *The Shapes of the Church to Come*, Kingsway, 2001

Neighbour, Ralph. *Where do we go from here?* Touch Publications, 1991

Nelson, Alan. *Leading Your Ministry*, Abingdon Press, 1996

Nelson, John (ed.). *Management and Ministry, appreciating contemporary issues*, MODEM, The Canterbury Press, 1996
Leading, Managing, Ministering – challenging questions for church and society, MODEM, The Canterbury Press, 1999

Newbigin, Lesslie. *The Household of God*, SCM, 1953

Noble, John. *The Shaking: turning the church inside out to turn the world upside down*, Monarch, 2002

Noll, Mark. *The Scandal of the Evangelical Mind*, Eerdmans, 1994

Pattison, Stephen. *The faith of the managers – when management becomes religion*, Cassell, 1997

Pelikan, Jaroslav. *The Christian Tradition I: The Emergence of the Catholic Tradition (100–600)*, University of Chicago Press, 1971

Perase, Meic and Matthews, Chris. *We must stop meeting like this!* Kingsway, 1999

Percy, Martyn. *Power and the Church – Ecclesiology in an age of transition*, Cassell, 1998
Salt of the Earth, Religious Resilience in a Secular Age, Continuum/Sheffield Academic Press, 2001

Peterson, Eugene. *Five Smooth Stones for Pastoral Work*, Eerdmans, 1980
Working the Angles: The Shape of Pastoral Integrity, Eerdmans, 1982

Under the Unpredictable Plant, an exploration in vocational holiness, Eerdmans, 1992

Potter, Phil. *The Challenge of Cell Church*, BRF and CPAS, 2001

Price, Peter B. *Seeds of the Word, Biblical Reflection for Small Church Communities*, DLT, 1996

Prior, David. *The Church in the Home*, Marshall, Morgan and Scott, 1983

Putnam, Robert. *Bowling Alone: The Collapse and Revival of American Community*, Simon and Schuster, 1999

Pytches, David. *Leadership for New Life*, Hodder and Stoughton, 1998

Rack, Henry D. *Reasonable Enthusiast, John Wesley and Rise of Methodism*, Epworth Press, 1992

Richter, Philip and Francis, Leslie. *Gone but not Forgotten – Church Leaving and Returning*, DLT, 1998

Ritzer, George. *The McDonaldisation of Society*, Pine Forge Press, 1993

Schillebeeckx, Edward. *Church – The Human Story of God*, SCM, 1989

Schwartz, Christian. *Natural Church Development*, British Church Growth Association, 1997

Paridigm Shift in the Church – How Natural Church Development Can Transform Theological Thinking, Churchsmart Resources, 1999

Seccombe, David. *Luke's Vision for the Church* in *A Vision for the Church* in *Studies in Early Christian Ecclesiology in honour of J.P.M. Swete*, edited by Markus Bockmuehl and Michael Thompson, T & T Clarke, 1997

Senge, Peter M. *The Fifth Discipline: The Art and Practice of the Learning Organisation*, Doubleday/Currency Books, 1990

Simson, Wolfgang. *Houses that change the world – the return of the House Churches*, OM Publishing, 1998

Smith, Mark. *Religion in Industrial Society, Oldham and Saddleworth, 1740–1865*, Oxford Historical Monographs, Clarendon Press, 1994

Stevens, R. Paul. *The Abolition of the Laity – Vocation, Work and Ministry in Biblical Perspective*, Paternoster, 1999

Stockstill, Larry. *The Cell Church – Preparing your church for the coming harvest*, Regal Books, 1998

The Methodist Church. *Called to Love and Praise*, Faith and Order Committee, 1995

Tiller, John. *A Strategy for the Church's Ministry*, Church Information Office, 1983

Tiller, John with Birchall, Mark. *The Gospel Community and its Leadership*, Marshall Pickering, 1987

Torrance, Thomas F. *Service in Jesus Christ* in *Theological Foundations for Ministry*, ed. R. S. Anderson, T & T Clark, 1979

Van Gelder, Craig. *The Essence of the Church – a Community created by the Spirit*, Baker Books, 2000

Warren, Rick. *The Purpose Driven Church*, Bondservant, 1995

Warren, Robert. *In the Crucible*, Highland, 1988

On the Anvil, Highland, 1990

Building Missionary Congregations, Church House Publishing, 1995

Warren, Robert and Jackson, Bob. *There are Answers, Springboard Resource Paper 1*, Springboard, 2001 (4 Old Station Yard, Abingdon, Oxon)

Watson, David. *I believe in the Church*, Hodder and Stoughton, 1978

Widdicombe, Catherine. *Meetings that Work, A Practical Guide to Teamwork and Groups*, The Lutterworth Press, 1994, 2000

Wimber, John. *Power Evangelism*, Hodder and Stoughton, 1985
Power Healing, Hodder and Stoughton, 1986

Witherington III, Ben. *The Acts of the Apostles – A social-rhetorical commentary*, Eerdmans/Paternoster, 1998

World Council of Churches. *Baptism, Eucharist and Ministry*, WCC, 1982

Worsnop, Paul. *Facilitating Mission in British Methodist Churches, Lessons from historical and contemporary models*, MA thesis, University of Durham, 2000

Wright, Walter C. *Relational Leadership*, Paternoster, 2000

Zizioulas, John D. *Being as Communion, Studies in Personhood and the Church*, St Vladimir's University Press, 1985